A HOSPITAL CHAPLAIN'S GUIDE

Faith and Medicine

Dr. Maxwell Shimba

Printed in the United States of America

TABLE OF CONTENTS

INTRODUCTION

In the ever-evolving landscape of healthcare, the role of hospital chaplains has become increasingly vital. As we move towards a more holistic approach to patient care, the integration of faith and medicine has proven to be a significant factor in the healing process. This book aims to serve as a comprehensive guide for hospital chaplains, highlighting the critical intersection of spiritual care and medical treatment. By addressing the spiritual, emotional, and psychological needs of patients, chaplains contribute to the overall well-being and recovery of those they serve.

The Importance of Spiritual Care

Healthcare professionals now widely recognize that healing extends beyond the physical body. Patients often grapple with existential questions, emotional distress, and spiritual crises during their medical journeys. Hospital chaplains are uniquely positioned to address these aspects, providing a source of comfort, hope, and meaning. The presence of a compassionate chaplain can transform the healthcare experience, offering a sense of peace and support that complements medical interventions.

The Chaplain's Role in Modern Healthcare

Historically, hospital chaplaincy was primarily associated with Christian ministry. However, contemporary chaplaincy encompasses a diverse range of faith traditions and spiritual practices. This inclusivity allows chaplains to meet the varied spiritual needs of patients from different cultural and religious backgrounds. The modern hospital chaplain serves not only as a spiritual caregiver but also as an integral part of the multidisciplinary healthcare team. They collaborate with doctors, nurses, social workers, and other professionals to provide holistic care that respects the patient's spiritual and cultural values.

Goals of This Guide

This book is designed to equip hospital chaplains with the essential skills, knowledge, and competencies needed to navigate the complex healthcare environment. Whether you are a seasoned chaplain or new to the field, this guide offers valuable insights and practical tools to enhance your ministry. The goals of this guide include:

- Enhancing Spiritual Care: Providing strategies and techniques for conducting spiritual assessments, developing care plans, and offering effective spiritual interventions.

- Fostering Interfaith Competence: Encouraging a deep understanding of diverse religious traditions and cultural practices to offer respectful and inclusive care.

- Addressing Ethical Dilemmas: Offering frameworks and approaches for navigating ethical and moral challenges that arise in healthcare settings.

- Supporting Crisis Intervention: Equipping chaplains with the skills needed to respond to crises and provide trauma-informed care.

- Promoting Self-Care: Emphasizing the importance of self-care for chaplains to maintain their own well-being and resilience.

Structure of the Book

This guide is structured to provide a comprehensive overview of the various aspects of hospital chaplaincy. Each chapter focuses on a specific area of expertise, offering detailed information and practical advice:

1. The Role of a Hospital Chaplain: An exploration of the Chaplain's responsibilities, skills, and competencies.

2. Integrating Faith with Medical Care: Insights into the importance of spiritual care and models for integrating faith with medicine.

3. Spiritual Assessment and Care Planning: Techniques for conducting spiritual assessments and developing effective care plans.

4. Counseling Patients and Families: Approaches to providing emotional and spiritual support to patients and their loved ones.

5. Interfaith and Multicultural Competence: Strategies for understanding and respecting diverse faith traditions and cultural practices.

6. Ethical and Moral Dilemmas in Healthcare: Guidance on navigating ethical challenges in the healthcare setting.

7. Crisis Intervention and Trauma Support: Skills for responding to crises and providing trauma-informed care.

8. End-of-Life Care and Bereavement Support: Approaches to supporting patients and families during end-of-life care.

9. Self-Care for Chaplains: Emphasizing the importance of self-care and offering strategies for maintaining well-being.

10. Case Studies: Real-life scenarios illustrating the practical application of concepts discussed in the book.

The Journey Ahead

As you embark on this journey through the pages of this guide, we hope to inspire and empower you in your ministry. Hospital chaplaincy is a profound calling that requires compassion, empathy, and a deep understanding of the human spirit. By integrating faith and medicine, chaplains play a crucial role in the healing process, offering solace and support to those in need. We invite you to explore the chapters ahead, drawing on the wisdom and experiences shared to enhance your practice and make a meaningful impact in the lives of the patients and families you serve.

May this guide serve as a valuable resource in your journey as a hospital chaplain, enriching your ministry and deepening your ability to provide holistic care that embraces both faith and medicine.

Purpose and Goals

Purpose of This Guide

The purpose of this guide is to provide hospital chaplains with a comprehensive resource that addresses the multifaceted nature of their role in modern healthcare. As the landscape of medicine evolves, so too does the need for integrating spiritual care into patient treatment plans. This book seeks to bridge the gap between faith and medicine, offering chaplains the knowledge and tools they need to effectively support patients, families, and healthcare staff.

Chaplains serve as spiritual caregivers, counselors, and ethical advisors within the hospital environment. Their work is crucial in helping patients navigate the emotional and spiritual challenges that often accompany illness and hospitalization. This guide aims to deepen chaplains' understanding of their role, enhance their skills, and provide practical strategies for delivering holistic care that honors both the medical and spiritual dimensions of healing.

Goals of This Guide

The primary goal of this guide is to empower chaplains with the tools and understanding necessary to navigate the complex intersection of faith and medicine. The following specific goals outline the key areas of focus:

1. Enhancing Spiritual Care

- Conducting Spiritual Assessments: Teach chaplains how to conduct thorough spiritual assessments to identify the spiritual needs and resources of patients.

- Developing Care Plans: Guide chaplains in creating individualized spiritual care plans that address identified needs and integrate with overall medical treatment.

- Spiritual Interventions: Provide practical strategies and techniques for implementing spiritual interventions that promote healing and well-being.

2. Fostering Interfaith Competence

- Understanding Diverse Faiths: Educate chaplains about various religious traditions and spiritual practices to enhance their ability to provide inclusive care.

- Cultural Sensitivity: Promote cultural competence by encouraging chaplains to recognize and respect the cultural differences that influence patients' beliefs and healthcare decisions.

3. Addressing Ethical and Moral Dilemmas

- Navigating Ethical Challenges: Equip chaplains with frameworks and approaches for resolving ethical dilemmas commonly encountered in healthcare settings.

- Providing Ethical Guidance: Train chaplains to offer ethical guidance to patients, families, and healthcare staff, ensuring that care decisions align with moral principles and respect patient autonomy.

4. Supporting Crisis Intervention and Trauma Care

- Crisis Response: Prepare chaplains to effectively respond to crises, providing immediate spiritual and emotional support to those affected.

- Trauma-Informed Care: Teach chaplains the principles of trauma-informed care, enabling them to support patients and families experiencing trauma with sensitivity and compassion.

5. End-of-Life Care and Bereavement Support

- Comfort and Dignity: Guide chaplains in offering spiritual care that brings comfort and dignity to patients nearing the end of life.

- Bereavement Support: Provide strategies for supporting families through the grieving process, including facilitating religious rituals and offering emotional support.

6. Promoting Chaplain Self-Care

- Self-Care Strategies: Emphasize the importance of self-care for chaplains, offering practical strategies to maintain their own well-being and resilience.

- Preventing Burnout: Teach chaplains how to recognize signs of burnout and implement preventive measures to sustain their ability to care for others.

7. Practical Applications and Case Studies

- Real-Life Scenarios: Present case studies and real-life scenarios that illustrate the practical application of concepts discussed in the book, providing chaplains with concrete examples to learn from.

- Reflective Practice: Encourage reflective practice by prompting chaplains to consider how they might apply the lessons and strategies from these case studies in their own work.

The purpose and goals of this guide are centered on enhancing the capabilities and effectiveness of hospital chaplains. By providing a detailed exploration of the intersection of faith and medicine, this book aims to equip chaplains with the knowledge, skills, and confidence needed to offer comprehensive spiritual care. As chaplains navigate the complexities of modern healthcare, this guide serves as a valuable resource to support their ministry and enrich their practice, ultimately contributing to the holistic healing of patients and their families.

DR. MAXWELL SHIMBA

CHAPTER 01

THE ROLE OF A HOSPITAL CHAPLAIN

Hospital chaplaincy has a rich and diverse history, evolving significantly over the centuries. Its roots can be traced back to the early Christian church, where providing care for the sick was considered a fundamental expression of faith. In medieval Europe, monastic orders such as the Benedictines and the Hospitallers established infirmaries and hospitals, where monks and nuns provided both medical care and spiritual support to the ill and dying.

As healthcare systems developed and modernized, the role of the chaplain became more formalized. In the 19th and early 20th centuries, many hospitals, particularly those in Western countries, were founded by religious organizations, and chaplains were often clergy from the Christian tradition. Their primary role was to offer spiritual care to patients, pray with them, and administer sacraments.

In the latter half of the 20th century, the landscape of hospital chaplaincy began to shift. The increasing diversity of patient populations necessitated a broader, more inclusive approach to spiritual care. Today, hospital chaplaincy encompasses a wide range of faith traditions and spiritual practices, reflecting the pluralistic nature of contemporary society. Chaplains now come from various religious backgrounds, including Judaism, Islam, Buddhism, Hinduism, and secular spiritual traditions. This evolution has enriched the practice of chaplaincy, allowing it to meet the diverse spiritual needs of patients in a more inclusive and holistic manner.

Core Responsibilities

The role of a hospital chaplain is multifaceted and deeply integral to the overall care of patients. While the specific duties of chaplains may vary depending on the institution and patient population, several core responsibilities are universally recognized.

1. Providing Spiritual Care:

Chaplains offer spiritual support to patients, families, and staff, addressing spiritual and existential concerns that arise during illness and hospitalization. This includes offering prayers, facilitating religious rituals, and providing spiritual counseling.

2. Emotional Support:

Hospitalization can be a stressful and anxiety-inducing experience. Chaplains provide a compassionate presence, offering emotional support and a listening ear to patients and their loved ones. They help individuals process their feelings, fears, and hopes, providing comfort and reassurance.

3. Ethical Guidance:

Chaplains often serve as ethical advisors within the healthcare team. They help patients, families, and staff navigate complex ethical dilemmas, such as end-of-life decisions, issues of patient autonomy, and conflicts over treatment choices. By providing a moral and ethical perspective, chaplains contribute to thoughtful and compassionate decision-making.

4. Crisis Intervention:

In times of crisis, such as sudden illness, trauma, or death, chaplains are called upon to provide immediate spiritual and emotional support. They offer comfort and guidance, helping individuals cope with the shock and distress of the situation.

5. Facilitating Communication:

Chaplains act as intermediaries between patients, families, and healthcare providers. They help facilitate open and compassionate communication, ensuring that the spiritual and emotional needs of patients are considered in their care plans.

6. Interfaith and Multicultural Competence:

Given the diverse nature of modern patient populations, chaplains must be adept at providing spiritual care across different faith traditions and cultural backgrounds. They respect and honor the beliefs and practices of all patients, fostering an inclusive and respectful environment.

Skills and Competencies

The effectiveness of a hospital chaplain hinges on a unique set of skills and competencies that enable them to provide meaningful and compassionate care. These skills include:

1. Active Listening:

Chaplains must be skilled listeners, able to hear and understand the concerns, fears, and hopes of patients and their families. Active listening involves being fully present, empathetic, and nonjudgmental, creating a safe space for individuals to share their stories.

2. Empathy and Compassion:

Empathy and compassion are at the heart of chaplaincy. Chaplains must be able to connect with patients on a deep emotional level, offering genuine care and concern.

This helps build trust and rapport, which are essential for effective spiritual care.

3. Cultural Competence:

Chaplains must be culturally competent, understanding and respecting the diverse cultural backgrounds and religious beliefs of patients. This includes being aware of different religious practices, customs, and traditions, and being able to provide appropriate spiritual care within this context.

4. Ethical Decision-Making:

Chaplains often encounter complex ethical dilemmas and must be equipped to navigate these situations thoughtfully. This requires a strong foundation in ethical principles and the ability to facilitate discussions that consider multiple perspectives and values.

5. Crisis Management:

The ability to remain calm and composed in crisis situations is crucial for chaplains. They must be able to provide immediate support and guidance, helping individuals cope with acute distress and trauma.

6. Interpersonal Communication:

Effective communication is key to the role of a chaplain. This includes not only verbal communication but also non-verbal cues, such as body language and eye contact.

Chaplains must be able to convey empathy, understanding, and support through their interactions.

7. Self-Care:

Given the emotionally demanding nature of their work, chaplains must practice self-care to maintain their well-being and effectiveness. This includes setting boundaries, seeking supervision and support, and engaging in activities that promote personal renewal and resilience.

The Chaplain as a Member of the Healthcare Team

Hospital chaplains are integral members of the healthcare team, collaborating closely with doctors, nurses, social workers, and other healthcare professionals. Their unique perspective and expertise in spiritual care complement the medical and psychosocial care provided by other team members.

1. Collaborative Care:

Chaplains work collaboratively with the healthcare team to ensure that the spiritual needs of patients are addressed as part of their overall care plan. This involves regular communication and coordination with other team members, sharing insights and observations that may impact patient care.

2. Advocacy:

Chaplains often serve as advocates for patients, ensuring that their spiritual and religious needs are respected and honored. This may involve advocating for specific religious practices, such as dietary restrictions or rituals, within the hospital setting.

3. Education and Training:

Chaplains also play a role in educating healthcare staff about the importance of spiritual care and cultural competence. This includes providing training on topics such as spiritual assessment, religious diversity, and ethical decision-making.

4. Research and Development:

As the field of spiritual care continues to evolve, chaplains contribute to research and development efforts, exploring new approaches and best practices for integrating spiritual care into healthcare. This helps to advance the field and ensure that chaplaincy remains relevant and effective in meeting the needs of patients.

The role of a hospital chaplain is both challenging and deeply rewarding. Chaplains provide essential spiritual and emotional support to patients, families, and staff, helping to create a compassionate and holistic healthcare environment. By understanding the historical background, core responsibilities, and essential skills and competencies of hospital chaplaincy, chaplains can better navigate their complex and vital role within the healthcare team. This chapter sets the foundation for the comprehensive exploration of hospital chaplaincy that follows, offering a roadmap for chaplains to enhance their practice and make a meaningful impact in the lives of those they serve.

CORE RESPONSIBILITIES

Hospital chaplains play a crucial role in providing holistic care within the healthcare setting. Their core responsibilities encompass providing spiritual care, emotional support, and ethical guidance to patients, families, and staff. As integral members of the healthcare team, chaplains ensure that the spiritual needs of patients are met, contributing to their overall well-being and recovery. This chapter explores these core responsibilities in detail, highlighting the essential functions and skills required for effective chaplaincy.

Providing Spiritual Care

1. Conducting Spiritual Assessments

Spiritual assessments are fundamental to understanding the unique spiritual needs and resources of each patient. Chaplains use various tools and techniques to conduct these assessments, such as the FICA (Faith,

Importance, Community, Address) model. This process involves:

- Faith Identification: Determining the patient's religious or spiritual beliefs and practices.

- Importance and Influence: Understanding the significance of these beliefs in the patient's life and healthcare decisions.

- Community Support: Identifying the patient's spiritual support system, including religious communities and spiritual advisors.

- Addressing Needs: Discussing how the healthcare team can support the patient's spiritual needs.

2. Facilitating Religious Practices and Rituals

Chaplains ensure that patients can observe their religious practices and rituals within the hospital setting. This includes:

- Prayer and Meditation: Providing spaces and opportunities for patients to pray or meditate according to their faith traditions.

- Sacraments and Rites: Administering or facilitating access to religious sacraments and rites, such as communion, anointing of the sick, or last rites.

- Dietary Accommodations: Coordinating with dietary services to accommodate religious dietary restrictions and preferences.

3. Offering Spiritual Counseling

Spiritual counseling involves providing guidance and support to patients as they navigate their healthcare journeys. Chaplains help patients explore existential questions, find meaning in their experiences, and draw on their spiritual resources for strength and comfort. This process includes:

- Active Listening: Creating a safe and supportive environment for patients to share their thoughts and feelings.

- Reflective Listening: Mirroring patients' concerns and emotions to validate their experiences.

- Providing Hope and Encouragement: Offering words of hope and encouragement that resonate with the patient's spiritual beliefs.

Offering Emotional Support

1. Supporting Patients

Hospitalization can be a challenging and anxiety-inducing experience for patients. Chaplains provide emotional support by:

- Being Present: Offering a compassionate and non-judgmental presence, simply being with the patient in their time of need.

- Addressing Fears and Anxieties: Helping patients articulate their fears and anxieties and providing reassurance and comfort.

- Encouraging Expression: Encouraging patients to express their emotions, whether through conversation, prayer, or other means.

2. Supporting Families

Families of patients often experience significant emotional stress as they support their loved ones through illness. Chaplains assist families by:

- Providing Information: Helping families understand the medical situation and the patient's needs from a spiritual perspective.

- Facilitating Communication: Mediating conversations between family members and healthcare providers to ensure that the family's concerns and wishes are heard and respected.

- Offering Bereavement Support: Supporting families through the grieving process, both during and after the patient's hospitalization.

3. Supporting Healthcare Staff

Healthcare professionals also face emotional challenges in their work. Chaplains support staff by:

- Offering Debriefings: Facilitating debriefing sessions after particularly stressful or traumatic events.

- Providing Counseling: Offering individual or group counseling sessions for staff members to address their emotional and spiritual needs.

- Promoting Self-Care: Encouraging healthcare staff to engage in self-care practices to maintain their well-being and resilience.

Providing Ethical Guidance

1. Navigating Ethical Dilemmas

Chaplains often encounter complex ethical dilemmas in the healthcare setting. They assist in navigating these challenges by:

- Mediating Discussions: Facilitating discussions among patients, families, and healthcare providers to explore the ethical dimensions of care decisions.

- Clarifying Values: Helping individuals clarify their values and beliefs to make informed and ethically sound decisions.

- Providing Ethical Frameworks: Offering frameworks and principles, such as autonomy, beneficence, non-maleficence, and justice, to guide decision-making.

2. Supporting End-of-Life Decisions

End-of-life care often involves difficult ethical decisions. Chaplains provide guidance and support in these situations by:

- Discussing Advance Directives: Helping patients and families understand and complete advance directives, such as living wills and durable powers of attorney for healthcare.

- Exploring Treatment Options: Facilitating conversations about the benefits and burdens of different treatment options, including palliative and hospice care.

- Offering Moral Support: Providing moral and spiritual support to patients and families as they make end-of-life decisions.

3. Advocating for Patient Rights

Chaplains advocate for the rights and dignity of patients by:

- Ensuring Informed Consent: Helping patients understand their treatment options and the implications of their choices, ensuring they can give informed consent.

- Respecting Autonomy: Advocating for patients' right to make their own healthcare decisions, respecting their autonomy and individual preferences.

- Addressing Discrimination: Identifying and addressing any instances of discrimination or bias in the provision of care.

The Chaplain as a Member of the Healthcare Team

1. Collaborative Care

Chaplains work collaboratively with the healthcare team to provide holistic care that addresses the physical, emotional, and spiritual needs of patients. This involves:

- Regular Communication: Maintaining open lines of communication with doctors, nurses, social workers, and other healthcare professionals.

- Integrating Care Plans: Ensuring that spiritual care plans are integrated into the overall care plan for each patient.

- Participating in Rounds: Joining medical rounds and team meetings to provide insights and updates on patients' spiritual needs.

2. Education and Training

Chaplains play a vital role in educating and training healthcare staff on the importance of spiritual care and cultural competence. This includes:

- Conducting Workshops: Offering workshops and seminars on topics such as spiritual assessment, religious diversity, and ethical decision-making.

- Providing Resources: Sharing resources, such as articles, books, and online materials, to enhance staff understanding of spiritual care.

- Mentoring and Supervision: Providing mentorship and supervision to other chaplains and spiritual care providers, fostering professional growth and development.

3. Research and Development

Chaplains contribute to the ongoing development of the field of spiritual care by engaging in research and development activities. This involves:

- Conducting Research: Participating in or leading research studies to explore the impact of spiritual care on patient outcomes and well-being.

- Publishing Findings: Sharing research findings through publications, presentations, and conferences to advance the knowledge base of hospital chaplaincy.

- Innovating Practices: Developing and implementing new approaches and best practices for integrating spiritual care into healthcare.

The core responsibilities of hospital chaplains are diverse and multifaceted, encompassing spiritual care, emotional support, and ethical guidance. By fulfilling these responsibilities, chaplains play a vital role in providing holistic care that addresses the comprehensive needs of patients, families, and healthcare staff. As integral members of the healthcare team, chaplains ensure that the spiritual dimension of healing is honored and respected, contributing to the overall well-being and recovery of those they serve. This chapter provides a foundation for understanding the essential functions of hospital chaplaincy, setting the stage for the detailed exploration of specific skills and practices in the chapters that follow.

SKILLS AND COMPETENCIES

The role of a hospital chaplain requires a diverse set of skills and competencies to effectively address the spiritual, emotional, and ethical needs of patients, families, and healthcare staff. This chapter delves into the essential skills and competencies that chaplains must develop and refine to provide holistic and compassionate care within the healthcare environment.

Active Listening

1. Definition and Importance

Active listening is a fundamental skill for hospital chaplains, involving fully engaging with and understanding the speaker's message. It goes beyond merely hearing words; it encompasses paying attention to the speaker's emotions, body language, and underlying concerns.

2. Techniques of Active Listening

- Attentive Body Language: Maintain eye contact, nod in acknowledgment, and use open body posture to show engagement.

- Paraphrasing: Reflect back on what the speaker has said in your own words to ensure understanding.

- Clarifying Questions: Ask questions to gain a deeper understanding of the speaker's message.

- Empathetic Responses: Respond with empathy, acknowledging the speaker's feelings and experiences.

3. Benefits of Active Listening

Active listening fosters trust and rapport between chaplains and those they serve. It helps patients feel heard and understood, which can alleviate feelings of isolation and anxiety. Additionally, it allows chaplains to gather important information that can guide their spiritual care interventions.

Empathy and Compassion

1. Definition and Importance

Empathy involves understanding and sharing the feelings of another person, while compassion involves a desire to alleviate their suffering. Both are crucial for hospital chaplains, as they help build a connection with patients and provide comfort and support.

2. Developing Empathy and Compassion

- Self-Reflection: Regularly reflect on your own emotions and experiences to better understand and relate to others.

- Mindfulness Practices: Engage in mindfulness practices to stay present and fully engaged with those you are serving.

- Continuing Education: Participate in training and workshops on empathy and compassion to enhance these skills.

3. Application in Chaplaincy

Empathy and compassion are applied in various aspects of chaplaincy, from providing emotional support to patients and families to offering comfort during crises. These skills enable chaplains to connect with individuals on a deeper level and provide meaningful, supportive care.

Cultural Competence

1. Definition and Importance

Cultural competence is the ability to understand, appreciate, and interact with people from diverse cultural backgrounds. In the healthcare setting, it involves recognizing and respecting the cultural and religious beliefs and practices of patients and their families.

2. Elements of Cultural Competence

- Cultural Awareness: Be aware of your own cultural beliefs and biases and how they may influence your interactions.

- Cultural Knowledge: Gain knowledge about different cultural and religious traditions, especially those represented in your patient population.

- Cultural Skills: Develop skills to effectively communicate and interact with people from diverse backgrounds.

- Cultural Sensitivity: Show respect and sensitivity towards cultural differences and be open to learning from others.

3. Strategies for Enhancing Cultural Competence

- Education and Training: Participate in cultural competence training programs and workshops.

- Engagement with Diverse Communities: Engage with diverse communities to gain firsthand experience and understanding of different cultures.

- Resource Utilization: Utilize resources such as cultural guides, interpreters, and community liaisons to enhance your cultural competence.

Ethical Decision-Making

1. Definition and Importance

Ethical decision-making involves making choices that align with ethical principles and values, particularly in complex and challenging situations. For chaplains, this often includes navigating dilemmas related to patient care, autonomy, and end-of-life decisions.

2. Ethical Principles in Healthcare

- Autonomy: Respecting the patient's right to make their own decisions.

- Beneficence: Acting in the best interest of the patient.

- Non-maleficence: Avoiding harm to the patient.

- Justice: Ensuring fairness and equity in the provision of care.

3. Ethical Decision-Making Frameworks

- Four Principles Approach: This framework involves considering the principles of autonomy, beneficence, non-maleficence, and justice in decision-making.

- Case-Based Approach: Analyzing specific cases to draw parallels and identify ethical solutions.

- Reflective Equilibrium: Balancing ethical principles and practical considerations to arrive at a well-reasoned decision.

4. Role of Chaplains in Ethical Decision-Making

Chaplains provide ethical guidance by facilitating discussions among patients, families, and healthcare providers. They help clarify values and beliefs, mediate conflicts, and support informed decision-making. Chaplains also advocate for the ethical treatment of patients and the protection of their rights.

Crisis Intervention and Trauma Support

1. Definition and Importance

Crisis intervention involves providing immediate and effective support during acute distress or emergencies. Trauma support addresses the emotional and psychological impact of traumatic events. Both are critical components of chaplaincy, as crises and trauma are common in healthcare settings.

2. Skills for Crisis Intervention

- Staying Calm: Maintain composure and provide a calming presence during a crisis.

- Immediate Support: Offer immediate emotional and spiritual support to individuals in crisis.

- Assessment: Quickly assess the situation and the needs of those affected.

- Resource Mobilization: Connect individuals with additional resources and support services as needed.

3. Skills for Trauma Support

- Understanding Trauma: Recognize the signs and symptoms of trauma and understand its impact on individuals.

- Trauma-Informed Care: Provide care that acknowledges and respects the trauma experiences of individuals.

- Building Trust: Establish a trusting relationship to support healing and recovery.

- Long-Term Support: Offer ongoing support and follow-up care to help individuals process and cope with trauma.

The skills and competencies required for effective hospital chaplaincy are diverse and multifaceted. Active listening, empathy, cultural competence, ethical decision-making, and crisis intervention and trauma support are essential for providing holistic and compassionate care. By developing and refining these skills, chaplains can better serve patients, families, and healthcare staff, addressing their spiritual, emotional, and ethical needs in a meaningful and impactful way. This chapter provides a foundation for understanding the core competencies of hospital chaplaincy, setting the stage for the detailed exploration of specific practices and strategies in the chapters that follow.

CHAPTER 02

INTEGRATING FAITH WITH MEDICAL CARE

The Importance of Spiritual Care

Spiritual care is increasingly recognized as a critical component of holistic healthcare. It addresses the spiritual and emotional needs of patients, promoting overall well-being and recovery. By integrating faith with medical care, healthcare providers can offer a more comprehensive approach to healing that considers the whole person – body, mind, and spirit.

Understanding Spiritual Care

1. Definition of Spiritual Care

Spiritual care involves recognizing and responding to the spiritual needs of patients. It encompasses a range of activities, including providing emotional support, facilitating religious rituals, and helping patients find meaning and purpose in their experiences. Spiritual care is personalized, reflecting the individual beliefs and values of each patient.

2. Benefits of Spiritual Care

- Enhanced Well-Being: Patients who receive spiritual care often report higher levels of well-being and satisfaction with their care. They may experience reduced anxiety, depression, and stress.

- Improved Coping: Spiritual care helps patients cope with illness, pain, and uncertainty. It provides a source of strength and comfort, helping them navigate their healthcare journey.

- Better Health Outcomes: Research indicates that addressing spiritual needs can lead to improved health outcomes, including faster recovery times and better management of chronic conditions.

- Holistic Healing: By addressing the spiritual dimension of health, healthcare providers can offer more holistic care that considers the patient's entire experience.

Models of Integrating Faith with Medical Care

1. Biopsychosocial-Spiritual Model

The biopsychosocial-spiritual model is a comprehensive framework that considers the physical, psychological, social, and spiritual dimensions of health. This model recognizes that each aspect of a person's life contributes to their overall well-being and that addressing these dimensions holistically can enhance health outcomes.

2. Interdisciplinary Approach

An interdisciplinary approach involves collaboration among healthcare providers, including doctors, nurses, social workers, and chaplains. Each team member brings their expertise to address different aspects of the patient's care. Chaplains play a crucial role in this model by providing spiritual care and supporting the emotional and spiritual needs of patients and families.

3. Patient-Centered Care

Patient-centered care focuses on the individual needs and preferences of patients. It involves actively involving patients in their care decisions and respecting their values and beliefs. Integrating spiritual care into patient-centered care ensures that patients' spiritual needs are considered and addressed.

Implementing Spiritual Care in Healthcare Settings

1. Conducting Spiritual Assessments

Spiritual assessments help identify the spiritual needs and resources of patients. Tools like the FICA (Faith, Importance, Community, Address) model can guide healthcare providers in conducting these assessments. Key components include:

- Faith Identification: Determining the patient's religious or spiritual beliefs and practices.

- Importance and Influence: Understanding the significance of these beliefs in the patient's life and healthcare decisions.

- Community Support: Identifying the patient's spiritual support system, including religious communities and spiritual advisors.

- Addressing Needs: Discussing how the healthcare team can support the patient's spiritual needs.

2. Developing Spiritual Care Plans

Based on the spiritual assessment, healthcare providers can develop individualized spiritual care plans. These plans outline specific interventions and support strategies tailored to the patient's needs. Components of a spiritual care plan may include:

- Prayer and Meditation: Providing opportunities for patients to engage in prayer or meditation according to their faith traditions.

- Religious Rituals: Facilitating access to religious rituals and sacraments, such as communion, anointing of the sick, or last rites.

- Counseling and Support: Offering spiritual counseling and emotional support to help patients cope with their illness and find meaning in their experiences.

- Community Involvement: Involving the patient's religious community or spiritual advisors in their care, if desired.

3. Training Healthcare Staff

To effectively integrate spiritual care into healthcare, it is essential to train healthcare staff on the importance of spiritual care and how to provide it. Training programs should cover:

- Understanding Spirituality: Educating staff on the concept of spirituality and its role in health and healing.

- Conducting Assessments: Teaching staff how to conduct spiritual assessments and identify patients' spiritual needs.

Cultural Competence: Enhancing cultural competence to respect and honor the diverse spiritual and religious beliefs of patients.

- Communication Skills: Developing communication skills to discuss spiritual matters sensitively and respectfully.

4. Creating a Supportive Environment

Healthcare settings should create an environment that supports spiritual care. This includes:

Designated Spaces: Providing designated spaces for prayer, meditation, and quiet reflection.

- Accessible Resources: Making religious texts, prayer books, and spiritual resources available to patients and families.

- Inclusive Policies: Develop policies that support the provision of spiritual care and respect the religious and spiritual needs of patients.

Collaboration with Healthcare Providers

1. Building Relationships

Chaplains must build strong relationships with other healthcare providers to effectively integrate spiritual care into patient care. This involves:

- Regular Communication: Maintaining open and regular communication with doctors, nurses, and other team members.

- Collaborative Care Planning: Participating in care planning meetings to ensure that spiritual care is included in the overall care plan.

- Advocacy: Advocating for the spiritual needs of patients within the healthcare team.

2. Providing Education and Support

Chaplains can provide education and support to healthcare providers to enhance their understanding of spiritual care. This includes:

- Workshops and Seminars: Offering workshops and seminars on spiritual care, cultural competence, and ethical decision-making.

- Resource Sharing: Providing resources, such as articles, books, and online materials, to support ongoing education.

- One-on-One Support: Offering one-on-one support and consultation to healthcare providers as needed.

Case Studies and Examples

1. Case Study: Integrating Faith in Palliative Care

In a palliative care unit, a chaplain works closely with the healthcare team to provide comprehensive care for a terminally ill patient. The chaplain conducts a spiritual assessment, identifies the patient's need for religious rituals, and coordinates with the patient's religious community to provide ongoing support. The integration of spiritual care helps the patient find peace and meaning during their final days, enhancing their overall well-being.

2. Case Study: Supporting a Family through Crisis

A family is struggling with the sudden illness of a loved one. The chaplain provides immediate emotional and spiritual support, facilitating open communication among family members and healthcare providers. The chaplain helps the family navigate their religious beliefs and practices, offering comfort and guidance. This support helps the family cope with the crisis and make informed decisions about their loved one's care.

Integrating faith with medical care is essential for providing holistic healthcare that addresses the spiritual, emotional, and physical needs of patients. By recognizing the importance of spiritual care and implementing effective strategies for its integration, healthcare providers can enhance patient well-being and promote holistic healing. This chapter has explored the key components of integrating faith with medical care, including understanding spiritual care, implementing spiritual care practices, collaborating with healthcare providers, and providing education and support. As we move forward, it is crucial to continue prioritizing spiritual care as an integral part of healthcare, ensuring that patients receive the comprehensive and compassionate care they deserve.

MODELS OF INTEGRATION

Integrating faith and medicine involves incorporating spiritual care into the overall healthcare framework to address the comprehensive needs of patients. Various models exist to guide this integration, each offering a unique approach to considering the physical, psychological, social, and spiritual dimensions of health. This chapter explores several key models of integration, including the biopsychosocial-spiritual model, the interdisciplinary approach, and the patient-centered care model. Understanding these models helps healthcare providers effectively incorporate spiritual care into their practice, ensuring holistic patient care.

Biopsychosocial-Spiritual Model

1. Definition and Components

The biopsychosocial-spiritual model is a comprehensive framework that expands the traditional biopsychosocial model by adding a spiritual dimension. This model recognizes that health and well-being are influenced by four interconnected domains:

- Biological: Physical health and medical conditions.

- Psychological: Mental and emotional health.

- Social: Interpersonal relationships and social support.

- Spiritual: Beliefs, values, and spiritual practices.

2. Importance of the Spiritual Dimension

The spiritual dimension is crucial because it encompasses the beliefs, values, and practices that give individuals a sense of meaning and purpose. Addressing this dimension can enhance overall well-being and support the healing process, particularly during times of illness and crisis.

3. Application in Healthcare

Implementing the biopsychosocial-spiritual model involves:

- Comprehensive Assessments: Conducting assessments that address all four dimensions of health, including spiritual assessments.

- Integrated Care Plans: Developing care plans that incorporate interventions for physical, psychological, social, and spiritual needs.

- Collaborative Team Approach: Ensuring that healthcare providers from different disciplines, including chaplains, work together to provide holistic care.

4. Case Example

A patient with a chronic illness is struggling with depression and social isolation. Using the biopsychosocial-spiritual model, the healthcare team conducts a comprehensive assessment, identifying the patient's physical health needs, psychological challenges, lack of social support, and spiritual distress. The care plan includes medical treatment, counseling, social support services, and spiritual care interventions, leading to improved overall well-being.

Interdisciplinary Approach

1. Definition and Components

The interdisciplinary approach involves collaboration among healthcare providers from different disciplines to address the multifaceted needs of patients. This model emphasizes the importance of teamwork and communication to ensure that all aspects of a patient's health are considered.

2. Role of the Chaplain

In the interdisciplinary approach, chaplains play a vital role by providing spiritual care and supporting the emotional and spiritual needs of patients and families. They work alongside doctors, nurses, social workers, and other healthcare professionals to offer comprehensive care.

3. Benefits of Interdisciplinary Collaboration

- Holistic Care: By incorporating multiple perspectives, the interdisciplinary approach ensures that care is holistic and addresses all dimensions of health.

- Enhanced Communication: Regular communication among team members enhances understanding and coordination, improving patient outcomes.

- Shared Decision-Making: Collaborative care planning involves patients and their families in decision-making, ensuring that care aligns with their values and preferences.

4. Implementation Strategies

- Team Meetings: Regular interdisciplinary team meetings to discuss patient care plans and progress.

- Clear Communication: Establishing clear communication channels among team members to share information and updates.

- Respect for Roles: Recognizing and respecting the unique contributions of each team member, including chaplains.

5. Case Example

A patient in the intensive care unit requires complex medical care and emotional support. The interdisciplinary team, including doctors, nurses, social workers, and a chaplain, meets regularly to discuss the patient's condition and care plan. The chaplain provides spiritual support and facilitates communication between the patient, family, and healthcare providers, ensuring that the patient's spiritual needs are addressed alongside their medical treatment.

Patient-Centered Care Model

1. Definition and Components

The patient-centered care model focuses on the individual needs and preferences of patients. It emphasizes the active involvement of patients in their care decisions and respects their values and beliefs. Spiritual care is an integral part of patient-centered care, ensuring that patients' spiritual needs are considered and addressed.

2. Core Principles

- Respect for Patients' Preferences: Healthcare providers respect and honor the individual preferences, values, and beliefs of patients.

- Involvement in Decision-Making: Patients are actively involved in decisions about their care, ensuring that their voices are heard.

- Holistic Approach: Care is holistic, addressing physical, emotional, social, and spiritual needs.

3. Benefits of Patient-Centered Care

- Improved Patient Satisfaction: Patients who are involved in their care decisions and whose spiritual needs are addressed report higher levels of satisfaction.

- Better Health Outcomes: Patient-centered care is associated with better health outcomes, as patients are more likely to adhere to treatment plans that align with their values and preferences.

- Enhanced Trust: Building trust between patients and healthcare providers by respecting and honoring patients' beliefs and preferences.

4. Implementation Strategies

- Spiritual Care Assessments: Conducting spiritual care assessments as part of the overall patient assessment process.

- Individualized Care Plans: Developing individualized care plans that reflect patients' spiritual needs and preferences.

- Patient Education: Educating patients about their care options and involving them in decision-making processes.

5. Case Example

A patient with a life-threatening illness expresses a desire for spiritual support and guidance. The healthcare team conducts a spiritual care assessment and involves the patient in developing a care plan that includes spiritual counseling, religious rituals, and support from their faith community. By respecting the patient's spiritual needs and preferences, the team enhances the patient's overall well-being and satisfaction with their care.

Other Models of Integration

1. Integrative Medicine

Integrative medicine combines conventional medical treatments with complementary and alternative therapies, including spiritual practices. This model recognizes the value of integrating different healing modalities to address the comprehensive needs of patients.

2. Whole-Person Care

Whole-person care emphasizes treating the patient as a whole, considering all aspects of their life, including physical, emotional, social, and spiritual dimensions. This model aligns closely with the biopsychosocial-spiritual approach and promotes holistic healing.

3. Palliative Care

Palliative care focuses on providing relief from the symptoms and stress of serious illness. It involves an interdisciplinary approach that includes spiritual care as a core component, recognizing the importance of addressing spiritual distress and providing comfort and support to patients and families.

Conclusion

Integrating faith with medical care is essential for providing holistic healthcare that addresses the comprehensive needs of patients. Various models, including the biopsychosocial-spiritual model, the interdisciplinary approach, and the patient-centered care model, offer frameworks for effectively incorporating spiritual care into healthcare practice. By understanding and implementing these models, healthcare providers can enhance patient well-being, improve health outcomes, and ensure that care is compassionate, respectful, and inclusive. This chapter has explored the key models of integration, providing a foundation for further exploration of strategies and practices in the chapters that follow.

COLLABORATION WITH HEALTHCARE PROVIDERS

Effective collaboration with healthcare providers, including doctors, nurses, and other professionals, is essential for integrating spiritual care into the overall healthcare framework. Chaplains must communicate clearly and work as part of a multidisciplinary team to ensure that the spiritual needs of patients are met. This chapter explores the principles and practices of collaboration, highlighting the importance of teamwork, communication, and mutual respect in providing holistic patient care.

Principles of Effective Collaboration

1. Mutual Respect

Mutual respect is the foundation of effective collaboration. Healthcare providers must recognize and value the unique contributions of each team member, including chaplains. Respectful interactions foster a positive team dynamic and enhance patient care.

2. Clear Communication

Clear communication is crucial for successful collaboration. Chaplains must communicate effectively with other healthcare providers to share information, discuss care plans, and coordinate interventions. This involves:

- Active Listening: Paying attention to the perspectives and insights of other team members.

- Timely Updates: Providing timely updates on patients' spiritual needs and care interventions.

- Clarifying Expectations: Ensuring that all team members understand their roles and responsibilities.

3. Shared Goals

Collaborative care is guided by shared goals that prioritize the well-being of patients. Chaplains and healthcare providers work together to develop and implement care plans that address the physical, emotional, social, and spiritual needs of patients.

4. Interdisciplinary Teamwork

Interdisciplinary teamwork involves healthcare providers from different disciplines working together to provide comprehensive care. Chaplains play a vital role in this team, offering spiritual care and support that complements medical and psychosocial interventions.

Strategies for Effective Collaboration

1. Building Relationships

Building strong relationships with other healthcare providers is essential for effective collaboration. This involves:

- Engaging in Team Activities: Participating in team meetings, rounds, and other collaborative activities.

- Fostering Trust: Developing trust through consistent, reliable, and respectful interactions.

- Offering Support: Providing support and assistance to team members as needed, demonstrating a commitment to teamwork.

2. Participating in Care Planning

Chaplains should actively participate in care planning to ensure that spiritual care is integrated into the overall care plan. This involves:

- Attending Care Conferences: Joining care conferences and multidisciplinary meetings to discuss patient care plans.

- Contributing Insights: Sharing insights and observations about patients' spiritual needs and preferences.

- Collaborating on Interventions: Working with other team members to develop and implement interventions that address spiritual care needs.

3. Educating Healthcare Providers

Educating healthcare providers about the importance of spiritual care and the role of chaplains can enhance collaboration. This involves:

- Providing Training: Offering training sessions and workshops on spiritual care, cultural competence, and ethical decision-making.

- Sharing Resources: Distributing resources, such as articles, books, and online materials, to support ongoing education.

- Demonstrating Impact: Highlighting the positive impact of spiritual care on patient well-being and health outcomes.

4. Advocating for Spiritual Care

Chaplains must advocate for the inclusion of spiritual care in patient care plans and healthcare policies. This involves:

- Promoting Awareness: Raising awareness about the importance of spiritual care among healthcare providers and administrators.

- Supporting Policies: Supporting policies and practices that prioritize and integrate spiritual care in healthcare settings.

- Engaging in Research: Participating in research to demonstrate the benefits of spiritual care and inform best practices.

Case Studies of Effective Collaboration

1. Case Study: Integrative Cancer Care

In an integrative cancer care center, a chaplain collaborates with oncologists, nurses, social workers, and complementary therapy practitioners to provide holistic care for cancer patients. The chaplain participates in weekly multidisciplinary meetings, sharing insights about patients' spiritual needs and contributing to care plans. By fostering strong relationships and clear communication, the team ensures that patients receive comprehensive support that addresses their physical, emotional, social, and spiritual well-being.

2. Case Study: Pediatric Palliative Care

A pediatric palliative care team includes a chaplain, pediatricians, nurses, social workers, and child life specialists. The chaplain plays a crucial role in supporting children with life-limiting conditions and their families. The team meets regularly to discuss care plans, and the chaplain provides insights into the spiritual and emotional needs of patients and families. By collaborating closely with other team members, the chaplain helps create a supportive and compassionate environment for patients and their families.

3. Case Study: Emergency Department Crisis Intervention

In a busy emergency department, a chaplain works alongside doctors, nurses, and mental health professionals to provide crisis intervention for patients experiencing acute distress. The chaplain responds to calls from the medical team, offering immediate spiritual and emotional support to patients and families. By maintaining clear communication and collaborating on intervention strategies, the chaplain and healthcare providers ensure that patients receive timely and comprehensive care during crises.

Overcoming Challenges in Collaboration

1. Addressing Misunderstandings

Misunderstandings about the role of chaplains and the importance of spiritual care can hinder collaboration. Addressing these misunderstandings involves:

- Providing Clarity: Clearly explaining the role and contributions of chaplains to other healthcare providers.

- Sharing Success Stories: Highlighting examples of successful collaboration and the positive impact of spiritual care.

- Engaging in Dialogue: Engaging in open and respectful dialogue to address any concerns or misconceptions.

2. Navigating Ethical Dilemmas

Collaborative care often involves navigating complex ethical dilemmas. Chaplains can support ethical decision-making by:

- Facilitating Discussions: Facilitating discussions among patients, families, and healthcare providers to explore ethical dimensions of care decisions.

- Offering Ethical Guidance: Providing ethical guidance and frameworks to support decision-making.

- Advocating for Patient Rights: Advocating for the rights and dignity of patients, ensuring that their values and preferences are respected.

3. Balancing Workloads

Balancing workloads and responsibilities can be challenging for chaplains and other healthcare providers. Strategies for managing workloads include:

- Setting Priorities: Prioritizing tasks and focusing on the most urgent and important needs.

- Delegating Tasks: Delegating tasks to other team members or support staff as appropriate.

- Seeking Support: Seeking support from supervisors, peers, and professional networks to manage stress and prevent burnout.

Conclusion

Effective collaboration with healthcare providers is essential for integrating spiritual care into the overall healthcare framework. By building strong relationships, participating in care planning, educating healthcare providers, and advocating for spiritual care, chaplains can enhance their collaboration with doctors, nurses, and other professionals. Overcoming challenges in collaboration involves addressing misunderstandings, navigating ethical dilemmas, and balancing workloads. This chapter has explored the principles and practices of effective collaboration, highlighting the importance of teamwork, communication, and mutual respect in providing holistic patient care. As we continue to prioritize spiritual care in healthcare settings, collaboration among healthcare providers will remain a cornerstone of comprehensive and compassionate care for patients and their families.

CHAPTER 03

SPIRITUAL ASSESSMENT AND CARE PLANNING

Conducting a thorough spiritual assessment is crucial for understanding a patient's spiritual needs and resources. Spiritual assessments help healthcare providers develop personalized care plans that address the spiritual dimension of health. This chapter explores the importance of spiritual assessments, introduces various tools and models, and provides practical guidelines for conducting assessments and developing spiritual care plans.

The Importance of Spiritual Assessment

1. Understanding Spiritual Needs

Spiritual assessments help healthcare providers understand the spiritual needs of patients. These needs may include the desire for meaning, purpose, hope, and connection with a higher power or religious community.

Identifying these needs allows chaplains to offer targeted support and interventions.

2. Enhancing Patient Care

By addressing the spiritual dimension of health, spiritual assessments contribute to holistic patient care. They ensure that the care plan encompasses the physical, emotional, social, and spiritual aspects of the patient's well-being.

3. Building Trust and Rapport

Conducting a spiritual assessment can help build trust and rapport between patients and healthcare providers. It demonstrates a commitment to understanding and respecting the patient's beliefs and values, fostering a supportive and compassionate environment.

Tools for Conducting Spiritual Assessments

1. FICA Model

The FICA (Faith, Importance, Community, Address) model is a widely used tool for conducting spiritual assessments. It consists of four components:

- Faith: Exploring the patient's spiritual beliefs and practices.

- Importance: Understanding the significance of these beliefs in the patient's life.

- Community: Identifying the patient's spiritual support system, including religious communities and spiritual advisors.

- Address: Discuss how the healthcare team can support the patient's spiritual needs.

2. HOPE Model

The HOPE model is another effective tool for spiritual assessment. It includes the following components:

- H - Sources of Hope: Identifying what gives the patient hope, strength, comfort, and peace.

- O - Organized Religion: Exploring the role of organized religion in the patient's life.

- P - Personal Spirituality/Practices: Understanding the patient's personal spiritual beliefs and practices.

- E - Effects on Medical Care: Discuss how the patient's spirituality affects their healthcare decisions and needs.

3. SPIRIT Model

The SPIRIT model is a comprehensive tool that covers various aspects of spirituality. It includes:

- S - Spiritual Belief System: Exploring the patient's core spiritual beliefs.

- P - Personal Spirituality: Understanding the patient's personal spiritual experiences and practices.

- I - Integration and Involvement in a Spiritual Community: Identifying the patient's involvement in a spiritual or religious community.

- R - Ritualized Practices and Restrictions: Discussing any specific spiritual or religious rituals and restrictions.

- I - Implications for Medical Care: Understanding how spirituality influences the patient's medical care and decisions.

- T - Terminal Events Planning: Exploring the patient's wishes and needs related to end-of-life care and spiritual practices.

Conducting a Spiritual Assessment

1. Establishing a Connection

Building a connection with the patient is the first step in conducting a spiritual assessment. This involves:

- Creating a Safe Space: Ensuring that the patient feels comfortable and respected.

- Active Listening: Demonstrating genuine interest and empathy in the patient's experiences and beliefs.

- Non-Judgmental Attitude: Approaching the conversation with an open mind and without judgment.

2. Asking Open-Ended Questions

Using open-ended questions encourages patients to share their thoughts and feelings. Examples of open-ended questions include:

- "Can you tell me about your spiritual or religious beliefs?"

- "What gives you hope and strength during difficult times?"

- "Are there any spiritual practices that are important to you?"

- "How do your spiritual beliefs influence your healthcare decisions?"

3. Exploring Key Areas

The spiritual assessment should explore key areas such as the patient's faith, spiritual practices, community support, and the impact of spirituality on their healthcare. This involves:

- Faith and Beliefs: Understanding the patient's core spiritual beliefs and how they relate to their current situation.

- Spiritual Practices: Identifying any spiritual practices or rituals that are important to the patient.

- Community Support: Exploring the patient's involvement in a spiritual or religious community and the support they receive from it.

- Healthcare Impact: Discuss how the patient's spirituality affects their healthcare decisions and needs.

4. Documenting the Assessment

Documenting the spiritual assessment is essential for developing an effective care plan. This involves:

- Recording Key Insights: Noting the key insights and information gathered during the assessment.

- Communicating with the Healthcare Team: Sharing relevant information with other healthcare providers to ensure coordinated care.

- Updating the Care Plan: Incorporating the patient's spiritual needs and preferences into their overall care plan.

Developing a Spiritual Care Plan

1. Setting Goals and Objectives

The first step in developing a spiritual care plan is setting clear goals and objectives. These should be based on the insights gathered during the spiritual assessment and should reflect the patient's spiritual needs and preferences. Examples of goals and objectives include:

- Enhancing the patient's sense of hope and meaning.

- Facilitating access to spiritual or religious practices.

- Providing support during times of spiritual distress.

- Ensuring the patient's spiritual needs are considered in medical decision-making.

2. Identifying Interventions

Based on the goals and objectives, chaplains can identify specific interventions to address the patient's spiritual needs. These interventions may include:

- Prayer and Meditation: Providing opportunities for the patient to engage in prayer or meditation according to their faith traditions.

- Religious Rituals: Facilitating access to religious rituals and sacraments, such as communion, anointing of the sick, or last rites.

- Spiritual Counseling: Offering spiritual counseling and emotional support to help the patient cope with their illness and find meaning in their experiences.

- Community Involvement: Involving the patient's religious community or spiritual advisors in their care, if desired.

- Ethical Guidance: Providing ethical guidance and support for the patient's healthcare decisions.

3. Implementing the Care Plan

Implementing the spiritual care plan involves coordinating with the healthcare team and ensuring that the identified interventions are carried out. This includes:

- Collaborating with Healthcare Providers: Working with doctors, nurses, and other healthcare professionals to integrate spiritual care into the overall care plan.

- Monitoring Progress: Regularly monitoring the patient's progress and adjusting the care plan as needed.

- Providing Ongoing Support: Offering ongoing spiritual support to the patient and their family throughout their healthcare journey.

4. Evaluating Outcomes

Evaluating the outcomes of the spiritual care plan is essential for ensuring its effectiveness. This involves:

- Assessing Patient Satisfaction: Gathering feedback from the patient and their family to assess their satisfaction with the spiritual care provided.

- Measuring Well-Being: Evaluating changes in the patient's overall well-being, including their sense of hope, meaning, and emotional stability.

- Adjusting the Care Plan: Making any necessary adjustments to the care plan based on the evaluation results.

Case Studies and Examples

1. Case Study: Supporting a Patient with Chronic Illness

A patient with a chronic illness expresses a need for spiritual support. The chaplain conducts a spiritual assessment using the FICA model, identifying the patient's faith, importance of spirituality, community support, and specific needs. Based on the assessment, the chaplain develops a care plan that includes regular spiritual counseling, facilitating access to religious rituals, and involving the patient's faith community in their care. The patient reports increased hope and emotional stability, demonstrating the effectiveness of the spiritual care plan.

2. Case Study: End-of-Life Spiritual Care

A terminally ill patient and their family seek spiritual support during the end-of-life stage. The chaplain conducts a spiritual assessment using the SPIRIT model, exploring the patient's beliefs, rituals, community involvement, and end-of-life wishes. The chaplain develops a care plan that includes providing comfort through prayer and meditation, facilitating last rites, and offering bereavement support to the family. The patient and family express gratitude for the compassionate care, highlighting the importance of addressing spiritual needs at the end of life.

Conducting a thorough spiritual assessment and developing an effective spiritual care plan are essential components of holistic healthcare. By understanding and addressing the spiritual needs of patients, chaplains can enhance overall well-being, build trust and rapport, and provide meaningful support throughout the healthcare journey. This chapter has explored the importance of spiritual assessments, introduced various assessment tools and models, and provided practical guidelines for conducting assessments and developing care plans. As we continue to prioritize spiritual care in healthcare settings, these practices will remain crucial for ensuring comprehensive and compassionate patient care.

DEVELOPING A CARE PLAN

Developing a comprehensive care plan based on a thorough spiritual assessment is crucial for addressing the spiritual needs of patients. A well-crafted care plan includes specific interventions and support strategies tailored to the individual patient's needs and preferences. This chapter outlines the process of developing a care plan, setting goals and objectives, identifying appropriate interventions, implementing the care plan, and evaluating outcomes.

Setting Goals and Objectives

1. Identifying Patient Needs

The first step in developing a care plan is to identify the patient's spiritual needs, which have been gathered during the spiritual assessment. These needs might include finding meaning and purpose, connecting with a higher power, coping with anxiety or fear, and receiving support from their faith community.

2. Establishing Clear Goals

Goals should be specific, measurable, achievable, relevant, and time-bound (SMART). They provide direction for the care plan and help ensure that the interventions are effective. Examples of spiritual care goals include:

- Enhancing the patient's sense of hope and meaning.

- Providing opportunities for the patient to engage in spiritual or religious practices.

- Offering emotional and spiritual support during times of distress.

- Ensuring that the patient's spiritual beliefs are considered in medical decision-making.

3. Setting Objectives

Objectives are specific steps or actions that will help achieve the overall goals. They should be tailored to the patient's individual needs and preferences. Examples of objectives include:

- Facilitating weekly visits from the patient's spiritual advisor.

- Providing daily opportunities for prayer or meditation.

- Arranging for religious rituals or sacraments as requested by the patient.

- Offering regular spiritual counseling sessions.

Identifying Interventions

1. Spiritual Counseling and Emotional Support

Spiritual counseling is a core component of the care plan. It involves providing a listening ear, offering guidance, and helping the patient explore their spiritual beliefs and concerns. Key elements of spiritual counseling include:

- Active Listening: Providing a safe and supportive environment for the patient to share their thoughts and feelings.

- Reflective Responses: Helping the patient process their experiences by reflecting back their emotions and concerns.

- Offering Hope and Reassurance: Providing words of comfort and encouragement that align with the patient's spiritual beliefs.

2. Facilitating Religious Practices and Rituals

Many patients find comfort and strength in engaging in religious practices and rituals. The care plan should include specific interventions to support these practices, such as:

- Prayer and Meditation: Providing opportunities for the patient to pray or meditate according to their faith tradition.

- Sacraments and Rites: Facilitating access to religious sacraments and rites, such as communion, anointing of the sick, or last rites.

- Religious Texts and Materials: Ensuring that the patient has access to religious texts, prayer books, and other spiritual resources.

3. Community Involvement and Support

Involving the patient's spiritual or religious community can provide additional support and comfort. The care plan might include:

Visitation from Spiritual Advisors: Arranging for visits from the patient's pastor, priest, rabbi, imam, or other spiritual advisor.

- Connection with Faith Community: Facilitating communication between the patient and their faith community, such as through phone calls, video chats, or in-person visits.

- Support Groups: Connecting the patient with spiritual support groups or religious organizations that can offer additional support.

4. Ethical Guidance and Decision-Making Support

Chaplains can play a vital role in helping patients navigate ethical dilemmas and make informed healthcare decisions that align with their spiritual beliefs. This might include:

- Advance Directives: Assisting the patient in completing advance directives, such as living wills or durable powers of attorney for healthcare.

- Moral and Ethical Discussions: Facilitating discussions about the ethical dimensions of treatment options and helping the patient and their family make informed decisions.

- Advocacy: Advocating for the patient's spiritual and ethical preferences within the healthcare team.

Implementing the Care Plan

1. Collaboration with the Healthcare Team

Effective implementation of the care plan requires collaboration with the healthcare team. This includes:

- Regular Communication: Keeping open lines of communication with doctors, nurses, social workers, and other healthcare providers to ensure that spiritual care is integrated into the overall care plan.

- Interdisciplinary Meetings: Participating in interdisciplinary team meetings to discuss the patient's care plan and progress.

- Documentation: Documenting the spiritual care plan and any interventions in the patient's medical record to ensure continuity of care.

2. Providing Ongoing Support

Ongoing support is crucial for the success of the care plan. This involves:

- Regular Check-Ins: Scheduling regular check-ins with the patient to assess their spiritual needs and provide ongoing support.

- Adjusting Interventions: Being flexible and willing to adjust interventions based on the patient's changing needs and preferences.

- Continuous Monitoring: Monitoring the patient's progress and well-being, and making any necessary modifications to the care plan.

3. Engaging Family and Caregivers

Family members and caregivers can play a significant role in supporting the patient's spiritual needs. The care plan should involve:

- Family Meetings: Holding meetings with family members to discuss the patient's spiritual needs and the care plan.

- Providing Resources: Offering resources and guidance to family members on how they can support the patient's spiritual well-being.

- Encouraging Involvement: Encouraging family members to participate in spiritual practices and rituals with the patient.

Evaluating Outcomes

1. Assessing Patient Satisfaction

Evaluating the patient's satisfaction with the spiritual care provided is essential. This can be done through:

- Patient Feedback: Asking the patient for feedback on the spiritual care interventions and their overall experience.

- Surveys and Questionnaires: Using surveys or questionnaires to gather more structured feedback from the patient and their family.

2. Measuring Well-Being

Assessing changes in the patient's overall well-being is another important aspect of evaluating outcomes. This might include:

- Emotional Stability: Monitoring changes in the patient's emotional stability and levels of anxiety, depression, or distress.

- Sense of Hope and Meaning: Evaluating the patient's sense of hope, meaning, and purpose.

- Spiritual Comfort: Assessing the patient's sense of spiritual comfort and peace.

3. Adjusting the Care Plan

Based on the evaluation results, adjustments may be needed to improve the effectiveness of the care plan. This involves:

- Reviewing Goals and Objectives: Reviewing and, if necessary, revising the goals and objectives of the care plan.

- Modifying Interventions: Making modifications to the interventions based on the patient's feedback and changing needs.

- Continuous Improvement: Continuously seeking ways to improve the spiritual care provided, based on ongoing evaluation and feedback.

Case Studies and Examples

1. Case Study: Chronic Illness Care

A patient with a chronic illness is struggling with feelings of hopelessness and isolation. The chaplain conducts a spiritual assessment and develops a care plan that includes weekly spiritual counseling sessions, facilitating access to religious texts, and arranging for visits from the patient's faith community. Over time, the patient reports increased hope and emotional stability, demonstrating the effectiveness of the care plan.

2. Case Study: End-of-Life Care

A terminally ill patient expresses a desire for spiritual support during the end-of-life stage. The chaplain conducts a spiritual assessment and develops a care plan that includes daily opportunities for prayer, facilitating last rites, and providing bereavement support to the family. The patient and family express gratitude for the compassionate care, highlighting the importance of addressing spiritual needs at the end of life.

Developing a comprehensive care plan based on a thorough spiritual assessment is essential for addressing the spiritual needs of patients. By setting clear goals and objectives, identifying appropriate interventions, implementing the care plan, and evaluating outcomes, chaplains can provide meaningful and effective spiritual care. This chapter has outlined the process of developing a care plan, providing practical guidelines and case studies to illustrate best practices. As we continue to prioritize spiritual care in healthcare settings, these practices will remain crucial for ensuring holistic and compassionate patient care.

CHAPTER 04

COUNSELING PATIENTS AND FAMILIES

Counseling patients and families is a vital component of a hospital chaplain's role. Effective counseling involves using various techniques and approaches to provide emotional and spiritual support, particularly during times of crisis and grief. This chapter explores key counseling techniques such as active listening, reflective listening, and validation. It also delves into the specialized skills needed for crisis counseling and grief support.

Key Counseling Techniques

1. Active Listening

Active listening is the cornerstone of effective counseling. It involves fully engaging with the speaker, and paying attention to their words, emotions, and nonverbal cues.

- Definition and Importance: Active listening means being present in the conversation, showing empathy, and understanding the speaker's perspective.

- Techniques:

- Eye Contact: Maintain appropriate eye contact to show attentiveness.

- Nodding: Use nodding and other nonverbal cues to indicate understanding.

- Minimal Encouragers: Use brief verbal affirmations like "I see," "Go on," and "I understand" to encourage the speaker.

- Avoiding Interruptions: Allow the speaker to express themselves fully without interrupting.

2. Reflective Listening

Reflective listening involves mirroring back what the speaker has said to ensure understanding and validation of their feelings.

- Definition and Importance: Reflective listening helps clarify the speaker's message and demonstrates empathy and validation.

- Techniques:

- Paraphrasing: Restate the speaker's words in your own language to confirm understanding. For example, "It sounds like you're feeling overwhelmed by the diagnosis."

- Summarizing: Summarize longer conversations to ensure mutual understanding and identify key points.

- Reflecting Emotions: Reflect the speaker's emotions to show empathy, such as saying, "You seem really anxious about the surgery."

3. Validation

Validation involves acknowledging and accepting the speaker's feelings and experiences as legitimate.

- Definition and Importance: Validation helps the speaker feel heard and understood, reducing feelings of isolation and emotional distress.

- Techniques:

- Affirming Feelings: Acknowledge the speaker's emotions by saying, "It's understandable that you feel this way."

- Normalizing Reactions: Normalize the speaker's reactions by indicating that their feelings are common and expected in their situation.

- Avoiding Judgment: Refrain from judging or dismissing the speaker's feelings, even if they differ from your own perspective.

Crisis Counseling

1. Definition and Importance

Crisis counseling involves providing immediate and effective support to individuals experiencing acute distress or emergencies. Chaplains often encounter patients and families in crisis due to sudden illness, traumatic events, or the death of a loved one.

2. Key Skills and Techniques

- Staying Calm: Maintain a calm and composed demeanor to provide a stabilizing presence.

- Immediate Support: Offer immediate emotional and spiritual support to help individuals cope with the initial shock and distress.

- Assessing Needs: Quickly assess the individual's emotional and spiritual needs to provide appropriate interventions.

- Providing Information: Offer clear and concise information about the situation and available support resources.

3. Strategies for Effective Crisis Counseling

- Active Listening: Use active listening to understand the individual's immediate concerns and emotions.

- Empathetic Presence: Provide a compassionate and empathetic presence, allowing the individual to express their feelings without fear of judgment.

- Grounding Techniques: Use grounding techniques to help individuals manage acute anxiety or panic, such as deep breathing exercises or focusing on a specific sensory experience.

- Resource Mobilization: Connect individuals with additional support resources, such as mental health professionals, social workers, or community support groups.

4. Case Example

A family is in the emergency room after a car accident that resulted in severe injuries to a loved one. The chaplain provides immediate support by listening to their concerns, offering comforting words, and helping them navigate the medical process. The chaplain also connects them with a social worker for additional assistance and follows up to provide ongoing emotional and spiritual support.

Grief Support

1. Understanding Grief

Grief is a natural response to loss, encompassing a range of emotions such as sadness, anger, confusion, and guilt. Chaplains play a crucial role in supporting patients and families through the grieving process.

2. Key Components of Grief Support

- Providing a Safe Space: Create a safe and supportive environment where individuals can express their grief without fear of judgment.

- Acknowledging Loss: Validate the individual's experience of loss and acknowledge the significance of their feelings.

- Offering Comfort and Hope: Provide words of comfort and hope that align with the individual's spiritual beliefs and values.

3. Techniques for Supporting Grieving Individuals

- Active Listening: Use active listening to understand the individual's grief experience and emotions.

- Reflective Responses: Reflect the individual's feelings to show empathy and understanding.

- Normalization: Normalize the grief experience by explaining that their feelings are a natural response to loss.

- Rituals and Memorials: Facilitate religious or spiritual rituals and memorials that provide comfort and closure.

4. Long-Term Grief Support

Grief can be a long-term process, and ongoing support is often needed. Chaplains can provide long-term grief support by:

- Regular Check-Ins: Schedule regular follow-up meetings to provide ongoing emotional and spiritual support.

- Support Groups: Connect individuals with grief support groups where they can share their experiences and receive peer support.

- Resources and Referrals: Provide resources such as books, articles, and referrals to grief counselors or therapists.

5. Case Example

A patient in palliative care has recently passed away, leaving their family in deep grief. The chaplain meets with the family to provide emotional support, listens to their stories about the deceased, and facilitates a memorial service that honors their loved one's life. The chaplain continues to offer follow-up support through regular check-ins and connects the family with a local grief support group.

Addressing Ethical and Moral Dilemmas

1. Ethical Challenges in Counseling

Chaplains often encounter ethical and moral dilemmas in counseling, such as conflicts over treatment decisions, end-of-life care, and family disagreements.

2. Ethical Decision-Making Frameworks

- Four Principles Approach: Utilize the principles of autonomy, beneficence, non-maleficence, and justice to guide ethical decision-making.

- Case-Based Approach: Analyze specific cases to draw parallels and identify ethical solutions.

- Reflective Equilibrium: Balance ethical principles and practical considerations to arrive at well-reasoned decisions.

3. Role of Chaplains in Ethical Decision-Making

- Facilitating Discussions: Facilitate discussions among patients, families, and healthcare providers to explore ethical dimensions of care decisions.

- Providing Ethical Guidance: Offer ethical guidance and frameworks to support decision-making.

- Advocating for Patient Rights: Advocate for the patient's spiritual and ethical preferences within the healthcare team.

Counseling patients and families is a vital aspect of a hospital chaplain's role, requiring a range of techniques and approaches to provide effective support. Active listening, reflective listening, and validation are fundamental skills, while crisis counseling and grief support require specialized competencies. By understanding and applying these techniques, chaplains can offer meaningful and compassionate care, helping individuals navigate their emotional and spiritual challenges. This chapter has provided an in-depth exploration of counseling techniques and approaches, highlighting the importance of empathy, active listening, and ethical guidance in the provision of holistic care.

ADDRESSING SPECIFIC ISSUES

Chaplains often encounter a range of emotional and spiritual issues among patients and their families, including fear, anxiety, grief, and existential questions. Addressing these issues effectively requires a deep understanding of each and the ability to provide comfort, hope, and spiritual guidance. This chapter explores these specific issues in detail and outlines strategies and approaches that chaplains can use to support patients and families through their challenges.

Fear and Anxiety

1. Understanding Fear and Anxiety

Fear and anxiety are common responses to illness, hospitalization, and medical procedures. They can be triggered by uncertainty, concerns about prognosis, pain, and the loss of control.

- Fear: Often related to specific threats or dangers, such as a diagnosis, surgery, or the potential for death.

- Anxiety: A more generalized sense of unease or worry, often without a clear or immediate cause.

2. Techniques for Addressing Fear and Anxiety

- Active Listening: Allow the patient to express their fears and anxieties without interruption. Listen attentively and empathetically.

- Providing Information: Clarify medical information and procedures to reduce uncertainty and confusion.

- Grounding Techniques: Teach patients grounding techniques, such as deep breathing exercises, to help manage acute anxiety.

- Spiritual Practices: Encourage spiritual practices such as prayer, meditation, or reading religious texts that the patient finds comforting.

3. Offering Reassurance and Hope

- Reassuring Presence: Be a calming and reassuring presence, offering consistent support and understanding.

- Positive Affirmations: Use positive affirmations that align with the patient's beliefs to instill hope and confidence.

- Faith and Trust: Encourage the patient to draw on their faith and trust in a higher power or the medical team.

4. Case Example

A patient-facing major surgery expresses intense fear and anxiety about the outcome. The chaplain spends time listening to the patient's concerns, provides clear information about the surgical process, and prays with the patient for strength and protection. The chaplain also teaches the patient deep breathing exercises to help manage pre-surgery anxiety.

Grief and Loss

1. Understanding Grief

Grief is a multifaceted response to loss, encompassing emotional, physical, cognitive, and spiritual dimensions. It is a natural process but can be overwhelming and complex.

- Types of Loss: Patients may grieve the loss of health, independence, or loved ones. Families may grieve the impending or recent death of a loved one.

2. Techniques for Supporting Grief

- Creating a Safe Space: Provide a safe and supportive environment for patients and families to express their grief.

- Acknowledging Loss: Validate their feelings and acknowledge the significance of their loss.

- Reflective Listening: Reflect back their emotions to show empathy and understanding.

3. Facilitating Healing and Closure

- Rituals and Memorials: Facilitate religious or spiritual rituals and memorials that provide comfort and closure.

- Spiritual Counseling: Offer spiritual counseling to help individuals explore their grief and find meaning and hope.

- Connecting with Support Groups: Connect grieving individuals with support groups where they can share their experiences and receive peer support.

4. Case Example

A family is grieving the recent death of a loved one in the hospital. The chaplain meets with the family, listens to their stories about the deceased, and helps them plan a memorial service in the hospital chapel. The chaplain continues to provide follow-up support and connects the family with a local grief support group.

Existential Questions

1. Understanding Existential Questions

Patients often grapple with existential questions during times of illness and crisis. These questions may include concerns about the meaning of life, the nature of suffering, and what happens after death.

- Common Questions: "Why is this happening to me?" "What is the purpose of my life?" "What will happen to me after I die?"

2. Techniques for Addressing Existential Questions

- Exploring Beliefs: Encourage patients to explore their spiritual beliefs and how these beliefs inform their understanding of existential questions.

- Providing Perspective: Offer different spiritual or philosophical perspectives that may help patients find meaning and comfort.

- Normalizing Uncertainty: Acknowledge that it is normal to have unanswered questions and to seek meaning in times of crisis.

3. Offering Comfort and Meaning

- Personal Narratives: Help patients create a personal narrative that incorporates their experiences and beliefs, providing a sense of coherence and meaning.

- Spiritual Resources: Provide spiritual resources, such as religious texts, meditations, or prayers, that address existential concerns.

- Compassionate Presence: Be a compassionate and non-judgmental presence, offering support as patients navigate their existential questions.

4. Case Example

A patient with a terminal illness is struggling with questions about the purpose of their life and what will happen after they die. The chaplain listens to the patient's concerns, discusses their spiritual beliefs, and offers passages from religious texts that address the afterlife. The chaplain also encourages the patient to reflect on the meaningful relationships and achievements in their life.

Providing Comfort and Hope

1. The Role of Comfort and Hope in Healing

Providing comfort and hope is central to the role of a chaplain. Comfort helps alleviate emotional and physical distress, while hope provides a sense of possibility and optimism for the future.

- Comfort: Alleviating distress and providing a sense of peace and safety.

- Hope: Offering a sense of possibility, optimism, and future-oriented thinking.

2. Techniques for Providing Comfort

- Physical Comfort: Coordinate with healthcare providers to address physical discomfort and pain management.

- Emotional Comfort: Provide a supportive presence, empathetic listening, and reassurance.

- Spiritual Comfort: Offer prayers, blessings, or other spiritual practices that provide solace.

3. Techniques for Instilling Hope

- Positive Affirmations: Use positive affirmations and language that instills hope and confidence.

- Sharing Stories: Share stories of resilience and recovery that inspire hope.

- Faith and Spirituality: Encourage patients to draw on their faith and spiritual beliefs as sources of hope.

4. Case Example

A patient diagnosed with a chronic illness feels hopeless about their future. The chaplain spends time with the patient, listening to their concerns and providing emotional support. The chaplain shares stories of others who have managed similar illnesses and encourages the patient to find strength in their faith. Through regular visits, the chaplain helps the patient develop a more hopeful outlook.

Chaplains play a vital role in addressing specific issues such as fear, anxiety, grief, and existential questions. By using techniques such as active listening, reflective listening, and validation, chaplains can provide meaningful support to patients and families. Addressing these issues effectively involves understanding the underlying emotions, offering comfort and hope, and helping individuals find meaning and purpose in their experiences. This chapter has explored strategies and approaches for addressing these specific issues, highlighting the importance of empathy, compassion, and spiritual guidance in the provision of holistic care.

CHAPTER 05

INTERFAITH AND MULTICULTURAL COMPETENCE

In today's diverse and multicultural healthcare environment, chaplains must be knowledgeable about various religious traditions and spiritual practices. This understanding enables them to provide appropriate, respectful, and inclusive care to patients from different backgrounds. This chapter explores the importance of interfaith and multicultural competence, provides an overview of major world religions, and offers practical strategies for chaplains to enhance their cultural and religious literacy.

The Importance of Interfaith and Multicultural Competence

1. Enhancing Patient Care

Interfaith and multicultural competence are essential for providing holistic care that respects and honors the diverse spiritual needs of patients. By understanding and appreciating different religious traditions and cultural practices, chaplains can offer more personalized and effective support.

2. Building Trust and Rapport

Patients are more likely to trust and feel comfortable with chaplains who demonstrate cultural sensitivity and respect for their beliefs. This trust is crucial for building strong therapeutic relationships and providing meaningful spiritual care.

3. Promoting Inclusivity

An inclusive approach to spiritual care ensures that all patients, regardless of their religious or cultural background, receive the support they need. This promotes a sense of belonging and respect within the healthcare environment.

Overview of Major World Religions

1. Christianity

- Beliefs: Christians believe in one God and follow the teachings of Jesus Christ, who is considered the Son of God and Savior of humanity. The Bible is the sacred text.

- Practices: Common practices include prayer, reading the Bible, attending church services, and participating in sacraments such as baptism and communion.

- Key Holidays: Christmas (celebrating the birth of Jesus) and Easter (commemorating the resurrection of Jesus).

2. Islam

- Beliefs: Muslims believe in one God (Allah) and follow the teachings of the Prophet Muhammad, who is considered the final prophet. The Quran is the sacred text.

- Practices: Five Pillars of Islam include Shahada (faith declaration), Salat (prayer), Zakat (charity), Sawm (fasting during Ramadan), and Hajj (pilgrimage to Mecca).

- Key Holidays: Ramadan (month of fasting), Eid al-Fitr (festival marking the end of Ramadan), and Eid al-Adha (festival of sacrifice).

3. Judaism

- Beliefs: Jews believe in one God and follow the teachings of the Torah, the central reference of the Jewish religion. They also adhere to the teachings of the Talmud.

- Practices: Observing the Sabbath (Shabbat), prayer, reading the Torah, and following dietary laws (kosher).

- Key Holidays: Passover (celebrating the Exodus from Egypt), Yom Kippur (Day of Atonement), and Hanukkah (Festival of Lights).

4. Buddhism

- Beliefs: Buddhists follow the teachings of Siddhartha Gautama (the Buddha) and seek to achieve enlightenment (nirvana) through the Four Noble Truths and the Eightfold Path.

- Practices: Meditation, mindfulness, chanting, and participation in rituals and festivals.

- Key Holidays: Vesak (celebrating the birth, enlightenment, and death of the Buddha), and various local and regional festivals.

5. Hinduism

- Beliefs: Hindus believe in a supreme being (Brahman) manifested in many gods and goddesses. Key concepts include karma, dharma, and reincarnation.

- Practices: Worship (puja), meditation, yoga, and participation in festivals and rituals.

- Key Holidays: Diwali (Festival of Lights), Holi (Festival of Colors), and Navaratri (festival dedicated to the goddess Durga).

6. Sikhism

- Beliefs: Sikhs believe in one God and follow the teachings of Guru Nanak and the ten successive Sikh Gurus. The Guru Granth Sahib is the sacred text.

- Practices: Daily prayers, meditation on God's name, community service, and following the Five Ks (articles of faith).

- Key Holidays: Vaisakhi (celebrating the Sikh New Year and the formation of the Khalsa), and Guru Nanak's Birthday.

Practical Strategies for Enhancing Interfaith and Multicultural Competence

1. Continuous Learning

Chaplains should engage in continuous learning to deepen their understanding of diverse religious traditions and cultural practices. This involves:

- Reading and Research: Reading books, articles, and online resources about different religions and cultures.

- Workshops and Seminars: Attending workshops, seminars, and conferences on interfaith and multicultural topics.

- Formal Education: Pursuing formal education, such as courses or degrees in religious studies, theology, or cultural anthropology.

2. Building Relationships with Religious Leaders

Building relationships with local religious leaders and communities can enhance a chaplain's cultural competence. This involves:

- Networking: Networking with religious leaders from different faith traditions to learn from their perspectives and experiences.

- Community Involvement: Participating in interfaith and multicultural events and activities within the community.

- Inviting Collaboration: Inviting religious leaders to collaborate on educational programs and spiritual care initiatives.

3. Providing Inclusive Spiritual Care

Providing inclusive spiritual care requires sensitivity to the unique needs and preferences of each patient. This involves:

- Personalized Assessments: Conducting personalized spiritual assessments that take into account the patient's religious and cultural background.

- Respecting Preferences: Respecting the patient's preferences for spiritual practices, rituals, and dietary restrictions.

- Facilitating Access: Facilitating access to religious resources, such as sacred texts, prayer materials, and religious leaders.

4. Developing Cultural Competence Skills

Developing cultural competence involves building skills that enable chaplains to interact effectively with people from diverse backgrounds. This includes:

- Cultural Awareness: Being aware of one's own cultural biases and how they may affect interactions with others.

- Cultural Knowledge: Gaining knowledge about different cultural practices, values, and beliefs.

- Cultural Sensitivity: Showing respect and sensitivity towards cultural differences, and being open to learning from others.

- Cultural Adaptation: Adapting communication styles and interventions to be culturally appropriate and effective.

5. Addressing Language Barriers

Language barriers can hinder effective communication and spiritual care. Strategies for addressing language barriers include:

- Using Interpreters: Utilizing professional interpreters to facilitate communication with patients who speak different languages.

- Learning Key Phrases: Learning key phrases and greetings in the languages commonly spoken by patients.

- Providing Translated Materials: Providing translated spiritual care materials, such as prayers and religious texts, when possible.

Case Studies and Examples

1. Case Study: Providing Spiritual Care to a Muslim Patient

A Muslim patient requests spiritual support during their hospital stay. The chaplain, familiar with Islamic practices, arranges for a prayer mat and ensures the patient has a quiet space for daily prayers. The chaplain also contacts a local imam to visit the patient and provides resources about halal dietary options in the hospital.

2. Case Study: Supporting a Jewish Family

A Jewish family is dealing with the impending death of a loved one. The chaplain understands the importance of Jewish mourning practices and arranges for a rabbi to provide support. The chaplain also ensures that the family's dietary needs are met by coordinating with the hospital kitchen to provide kosher meals.

3. Case Study: Addressing the Needs of a Hindu Patient

A Hindu patient is facing a major surgery and expresses a desire for spiritual support. The chaplain provides access to sacred texts and arranges for the patient's family to perform a puja (worship ritual) in the hospital room. The chaplain also respects the patient's dietary restrictions and ensures that vegetarian meals are provided.

Interfaith and multicultural competence are essential for providing effective and respectful spiritual care in a diverse healthcare environment. By understanding diverse faiths, building relationships with religious leaders, and continuously developing cultural competence skills, chaplains can enhance their ability to support patients from various religious and cultural backgrounds. This chapter has explored the importance of interfaith and multicultural competence, provided an overview of major world religions, and offered practical strategies for chaplains to enhance their cultural and religious literacy. As we continue to prioritize inclusive spiritual care, these practices will remain crucial for ensuring that all patients receive the compassionate and respectful support they deserve.

CULTURAL SENSITIVITY

Cultural sensitivity is a crucial aspect of providing effective and respectful spiritual care in a diverse healthcare environment. Cultural competence involves recognizing and respecting cultural differences in beliefs, practices, and attitudes toward health and illness. This chapter explores the importance of cultural sensitivity, practical strategies for developing cultural competence, and techniques for providing culturally sensitive care to patients and their families.

The Importance of Cultural Sensitivity

1. Enhancing Patient Care

Culturally sensitive care improves patient outcomes by ensuring that care is tailored to the unique cultural and spiritual needs of each patient. This approach fosters a sense of respect and dignity, which is essential for holistic healing.

2. Building Trust and Rapport

Patients are more likely to trust and feel comfortable with healthcare providers who demonstrate cultural sensitivity. This trust is critical for effective communication, accurate assessment, and successful interventions.

3. Promoting Inclusivity

Cultural sensitivity promotes an inclusive healthcare environment where all patients feel valued and respected. This inclusivity helps create a supportive and healing atmosphere for patients from diverse backgrounds.

Developing Cultural Competence

1. Cultural Awareness

Cultural awareness involves recognizing and understanding one's own cultural biases and how they may affect interactions with others. It requires self-reflection and an openness to learning about other cultures.

- Self-Reflection: Reflect on your own cultural background, beliefs, and biases. Consider how these might influence your interactions with patients.

- Awareness of Biases: Acknowledge and address any biases or stereotypes you may hold about other cultures.

- Openness to Learning: Approach cultural differences with curiosity and a willingness to learn.

2. Cultural Knowledge

Cultural knowledge involves gaining information about different cultural practices, values, and beliefs. This knowledge helps healthcare providers understand the cultural context of patients' experiences and needs.

- Reading and Research: Read books, articles, and online resources about different cultures and their approaches to health and illness.

- Workshops and Training: Attend workshops, seminars, and training sessions on cultural competence and diversity.

- Engaging with Communities: Engage with diverse communities to gain firsthand experience and understanding of their cultural practices.

3. Cultural Sensitivity

Cultural sensitivity involves showing respect and understanding towards cultural differences. It requires adapting your approach to meet the cultural needs of patients and their families.

- Respect for Beliefs: Show respect for the cultural and religious beliefs of patients, even if they differ from your own.

- Effective Communication: Use culturally appropriate communication styles and avoid assumptions based on cultural stereotypes.

- Patient-Centered Care: Tailor your care to meet the cultural preferences and needs of each patient.

4. Cultural Adaptation

Cultural adaptation involves modifying your interventions and communication strategies to be culturally appropriate and effective. This ensures that care is relevant and meaningful to patients from diverse backgrounds.

- Adapting Interventions: Modify interventions to align with the cultural practices and preferences of patients.

- Using Interpreters: Utilize professional interpreters to facilitate communication with patients who speak different languages.

- Providing Resources: Offer culturally relevant resources, such as translated materials, religious texts, and information about local cultural practices.

Techniques for Providing Culturally Sensitive Care

1. Conducting Culturally Sensitive Assessments

Culturally sensitive assessments help identify the unique cultural needs and preferences of patients. This involves:

- Asking Open-Ended Questions: Use open-ended questions to explore the patient's cultural background and beliefs. For example, "Can you tell me about any cultural practices or beliefs that are important to you?"

- Listening with Empathy: Listen attentively to the patient's responses and show empathy for their cultural experiences.

- Respecting Preferences: Respect the patient's preferences and incorporate them into the care plan.

2. Building Relationships with Cultural Communities

Building relationships with local cultural communities can enhance your cultural competence and provide valuable resources for patient care. This involves:

- Networking with Community Leaders: Network with leaders from different cultural communities to learn about their practices and perspectives.

- Participating in Community Events: Attend cultural events and activities to gain a deeper understanding of different cultures.

- Collaborating on Initiatives: Collaborate with cultural communities on initiatives that promote cultural sensitivity and inclusivity in healthcare.

3. Adapting Communication Styles

Effective communication is essential for providing culturally sensitive care. This involves:

- Using Simple Language: Use simple and clear language to ensure that patients understand the information provided.

- Avoiding Jargon: Avoid medical jargon and technical terms that may be confusing or unfamiliar to patients.

- Being Mindful of Nonverbal Cues: Be aware of nonverbal communication cues, such as eye contact, body language, and personal space, which may vary across cultures.

4. Providing Culturally Relevant Resources

Providing culturally relevant resources helps ensure that patients have access to information and support that aligns with their cultural and spiritual needs. This involves:

- Translating Materials: Provide translated materials, such as informational brochures, consent forms, and spiritual care resources, in the patient's preferred language.

- Offering Religious Texts: Ensure that patients have access to religious texts and prayer materials that are relevant to their faith.

- Connecting with Cultural Services: Connect patients with cultural services, such as dietary accommodations, spiritual support, and cultural advocacy groups.

Case Studies and Examples

1. Case Study: Supporting a Buddhist Patient

A Buddhist patient is admitted to the hospital for surgery. The chaplain conducts a culturally sensitive assessment and learns that the patient practices meditation and follows a vegetarian diet. The chaplain arranges for a quiet space for the patient to meditate and coordinates with the hospital kitchen to provide vegetarian meals. The chaplain also provides a Buddhist prayer book and arranges for a local monk to visit the patient.

2. Case Study: Addressing the Needs of a Latino Family

A Latino family is coping with the hospitalization of a loved one. The chaplain recognizes the importance of family support in Latino culture and involves the extended family in discussions about the patient's care. The chaplain also arranges for a Spanish-speaking interpreter to facilitate communication and provides informational materials in Spanish.

3. Case Study: Providing Culturally Sensitive End-of-Life Care

A Native American patient is receiving end-of-life care. The chaplain learns that the patient values traditional healing practices and the presence of a spiritual leader. The chaplain arranges for a Native American healer to visit the patient and participate in traditional rituals. The chaplain also ensures that the patient's cultural and spiritual preferences are respected in the care plan.

Cultural sensitivity is essential for providing effective and respectful spiritual care in a diverse healthcare environment. By developing cultural competence through continuous learning, building relationships with cultural communities, and adapting communication styles and interventions, chaplains can enhance their ability to support patients from various cultural backgrounds. This chapter has explored the importance of cultural sensitivity, practical strategies for developing cultural competence, and techniques for providing culturally sensitive care. As we continue to prioritize inclusive spiritual care, these practices will remain crucial for ensuring that all patients receive the compassionate and respectful support they deserve.

CHAPTER 06

ETHICAL AND MORAL DILEMMAS IN HEALTHCARE

Ethical and moral dilemmas are common in healthcare settings, often involving complex decisions that impact patient care and outcomes. Chaplains play a crucial role in addressing these dilemmas by providing ethical guidance, supporting patient autonomy, and facilitating discussions among patients, families, and healthcare providers. This chapter explores common ethical issues in healthcare, the role of chaplains in navigating these dilemmas, and practical strategies for ethical decision-making.

Common Ethical Issues

1. End-of-Life Decisions

End of-life decisions are among the most challenging ethical dilemmas in healthcare. These decisions involve considerations about prolonging life, alleviating suffering, and respecting patient wishes.

- Life-Sustaining Treatments: Decisions about whether to initiate, continue, or withdraw life-sustaining treatments, such as mechanical ventilation, dialysis, or artificial nutrition and hydration.

- Palliative Care: Balancing the goals of palliative care, which focuses on comfort and quality of life, with curative treatments.

- Advance Directives: Respecting patients' advance directives, such as living wills or durable powers of attorney for healthcare, which outline their preferences for end-of-life care.

2. Patient Autonomy

Patient autonomy is the principle that patients have the right to make informed decisions about their own healthcare. Ethical dilemmas arise when there is a conflict between patient autonomy and other considerations, such as medical recommendations or family wishes.

- Informed Consent: Ensuring that patients have the information they need to make informed decisions about their treatment options.

- Refusal of Treatment: Respecting patients' right to refuse treatment, even if the decision may result in negative health outcomes.

- Decision-Making Capacity: Assessing and supporting patients' decision-making capacity, especially in cases involving cognitive impairment or mental illness.

3. Confidentiality

Confidentiality is a fundamental ethical principle that protects patients' privacy and personal health information. Ethical dilemmas arise when there is a need to balance confidentiality with other ethical considerations, such as protecting public health or ensuring patient safety.

- Sharing Information: Determining when it is appropriate to share patient information with family members, caregivers, or other healthcare providers.

- Mandatory Reporting: Navigating situations that require mandatory reporting, such as suspected abuse or infectious disease outbreaks, while maintaining patient confidentiality.

- Electronic Health Records: Ensuring the security and privacy of electronic health records and other digital health information.

The Role of Chaplains in Ethical Dilemmas

1. Mediating Ethical Discussions

Chaplains often serve as mediators in ethical discussions, helping to facilitate open and respectful communication among patients, families, and healthcare providers. This involves:

- Creating a Safe Space: Establishing a safe and supportive environment for discussing ethical concerns and differing perspectives.

- Active Listening: Listening attentively to all parties involved and validating their feelings and concerns.

- Clarifying Values: Helping individuals articulate their values and beliefs and understand how these influence their decisions.

2. Providing Ethical Guidance

Chaplains provide ethical guidance by offering frameworks and principles to support decision-making. This involves:

- Ethical Principles: Applying ethical principles such as autonomy, beneficence, non-maleficence, and justice to the decision-making process.

- Case Analysis: Analyzing specific cases to draw parallels and identify ethical solutions.

- Reflective Equilibrium: Balancing ethical principles and practical considerations to arrive at well-reasoned decisions.

3. Advocating for Patient Rights

Chaplains advocate for patients' rights, ensuring that their preferences and values are respected in the decision-making process. This involves:

- Empowering Patients: Empowering patients to express their wishes and make informed decisions about their care.

- Respecting Autonomy: Respecting patients' autonomy and supporting their right to make decisions about their own healthcare.

- Addressing Conflicts: Mediating conflicts between patients, families, and healthcare providers to ensure that patient rights are upheld.

Practical Strategies for Ethical Decision-Making

1. Ethical Decision-Making Frameworks

Using ethical decision-making frameworks can help guide the process and ensure that all relevant factors are considered. Common frameworks include:

- Four Principles Approach: Applying the principles of autonomy, beneficence, non-maleficence, and justice to the decision-making process.

- Case-Based Approach: Analyzing specific cases to draw parallels and identify ethical solutions.

- Reflective Equilibrium: Balancing ethical principles and practical considerations to arrive at well-reasoned decisions.

2. Facilitating Ethical Discussions

Facilitating ethical discussions involves creating a structured and supportive environment for exploring ethical dilemmas. This includes:

- Setting Ground Rules: Establishing ground rules for respectful and open communication.

- Encouraging Participation: Encouraging all parties to share their perspectives and feelings.

- Clarifying Information: Providing clear and accurate information about the medical and ethical aspects of the situation.

3. Documenting Ethical Decisions

Documenting ethical decisions is important for ensuring transparency and accountability. This involves:

- Recording Discussions: Keeping detailed records of ethical discussions and the decision-making process.

- Noting Rationales: Documenting the rationales for decisions made, including the ethical principles and considerations involved.

- Updating Care Plans: Ensuring that care plans are updated to reflect the decisions made and any changes in the patient's preferences or condition.

Case Studies and Examples

1. Case Study: End-of-Life Decision-Making

A patient with a terminal illness has expressed a desire to discontinue life-sustaining treatment and transition to palliative care. The patient's family is divided, with some members supporting the decision and others wanting to continue aggressive treatment. The chaplain facilitates a family meeting, listening to each person's perspective and helping the family understand the patient's wishes. The chaplain also provides ethical guidance based on the principles of autonomy and beneficence. Ultimately, the patient's wishes are respected, and the transition to palliative care is made with the family's support.

2. Case Study: Balancing Confidentiality and Safety

A patient with a history of mental illness confides in the chaplain about having suicidal thoughts but insists on keeping this information confidential. The chaplain faces an ethical dilemma between respecting the patient's confidentiality and ensuring their safety. The chaplain engages the patient in a discussion about the importance of safety and the need for appropriate support. With the patient's consent, the chaplain informs the healthcare team and ensures that the patient receives the necessary mental health intervention.

3. Case Study: Respecting Patient Autonomy

An elderly patient with cognitive impairment refuses a recommended medical procedure that could improve their quality of life. The healthcare team is concerned about the patient's decision-making capacity and the potential consequences of refusing treatment. The chaplain conducts a thorough assessment of the patient's decision-making capacity and facilitates a discussion with the patient and their family. The chaplain helps the patient articulate their values and preferences and ensures that the healthcare team respects the patient's autonomy while providing appropriate support and education.

Ethical and moral dilemmas are inherent in healthcare, often involving complex decisions that impact patient care and outcomes. Chaplains play a vital role in addressing these dilemmas by providing ethical guidance, supporting patient autonomy, and facilitating discussions among patients, families, and healthcare providers. By using ethical decision-making frameworks, facilitating ethical discussions, and advocating for patient rights, chaplains help navigate the complexities of ethical dilemmas and ensure that care is compassionate, respectful, and aligned with patients' values and preferences. This chapter has explored common ethical issues in healthcare, the role of chaplains in navigating these dilemmas, and practical strategies for ethical decision-making. As we continue to prioritize ethical and compassionate care, these practices will remain crucial for supporting patients and their families through difficult and challenging decisions.

ETHICAL DECISION- MAKING

Ethical decision-making is a crucial aspect of healthcare, especially when dealing with complex and challenging situations. Chaplains play a significant role in guiding patients, families, and healthcare providers through ethical dilemmas by using structured frameworks. This chapter explores various ethical decision-making frameworks, with a focus on the Four Principles Approach, and provides practical guidance for chaplains to resolve ethical dilemmas effectively.

The Four Principles Approach

1. Autonomy

Autonomy refers to the right of patients to make informed decisions about their own healthcare. Respecting autonomy involves acknowledging patients' preferences, values, and choices, and ensuring that they have the information and support they need to make informed decisions.

- Informed Consent: Ensuring that patients understand their treatment options and the potential risks and benefits.

- Respecting Refusals: Honoring patients' decisions to refuse treatment, even if it conflicts with medical advice.

- Supporting Decision-Making: Helping patients articulate their values and preferences and facilitating their decision-making process.

2. Beneficence

Beneficence involves acting in the best interest of the patient to promote their well-being. This principle requires healthcare providers to consider the potential benefits of treatment options and to act in ways that enhance the patient's health and quality of life.

- Promoting Well-Being: Taking actions that benefit the patient and improve their health outcomes.

- Balancing Benefits and Risks: Evaluating the potential benefits of a treatment against its risks and side effects.

- Providing Compassionate Care: Ensuring that care is compassionate and aimed at relieving suffering and improving quality of life.

3. Non-Maleficence

Non-maleficence is the principle of "do no harm." Healthcare providers must avoid actions that could cause unnecessary harm or suffering to patients. This principle emphasizes the importance of minimizing harm while pursuing beneficial outcomes.

- Avoiding Harm: Taking steps to prevent harm to patients, including avoiding unnecessary treatments or procedures.

- Risk Management: Identifying and mitigating potential risks associated with treatment options.

- Ethical Withdrawal: Making decisions about withdrawing or withholding treatment when it is no longer beneficial to the patient.

4. Justice

Justice involves ensuring fairness in the distribution of healthcare resources and treating patients equitably. This principle requires healthcare providers to consider the fair allocation of resources and to ensure that patients receive care based on their needs and circumstances.

- Fair Distribution: Allocating healthcare resources fairly and equitably among patients.

- Non-Discrimination: Ensuring that all patients are treated with equal respect and without discrimination based on race, gender, socioeconomic status, or other factors.

- Advocacy: Advocating for policies and practices that promote fairness and equity in healthcare.

Applying the Four Principles Approach

1. Case Analysis

The Four Principles Approach can be applied to analyze specific cases and guide ethical decision-making. This involves:

- Identifying Ethical Issues: Recognizing the ethical issues and conflicts present in the case.

- Applying Principles: Applying each of the four principles (autonomy, beneficence, non-maleficence, and justice) to evaluate the options and implications.

- Balancing Principles: Balancing the principles to arrive at a decision that respects patient autonomy, promotes well-being, minimizes harm, and ensures fairness.

2. Example Case: End-of-Life Decision-Making

A patient with advanced cancer expresses a desire to discontinue aggressive treatment and transition to palliative care. The healthcare team faces an ethical dilemma involving the patient's autonomy, the potential benefits and harms of continued treatment, and the fair allocation of resources.

- Autonomy: Respecting the patient's decision to discontinue treatment and ensuring they are fully informed about their options.

- Beneficence: Promoting the patient's well-being by focusing on comfort and quality of life through palliative care.

- Non-Maleficence: Avoiding unnecessary harm by not continuing aggressive treatment that may cause suffering without significant benefit.

- Justice: Ensuring that the patient receives fair access to palliative care resources and support.

By applying the Four Principles Approach, the healthcare team can arrive at a decision that respects the patient's wishes, promotes their well-being, minimizes harm, and ensures equitable access to care.

Other Ethical Decision-Making Frameworks

1. Case-Based Approach (Casuistry)

The case-based approach, or casuistry, involves analyzing specific cases to draw parallels and identify ethical solutions. This approach emphasizes practical decision-making based on previous cases and experiences.

- Comparative Analysis: Comparing the current case with similar cases to identify relevant principles and precedents.

- Practical Solutions: Focusing on practical solutions that address the specific circumstances of the case.

- Contextual Factors: Considering the unique context and details of each case to inform decision-making.

2. Reflective Equilibrium

Reflective equilibrium involves balancing ethical principles and practical considerations to arrive at a well-reasoned decision. This approach requires continuous reflection and adjustment to ensure that decisions align with ethical standards and practical realities.

- Balancing Principles: Weighing ethical principles against each other and against practical considerations.

- Continuous Reflection: Engaging in ongoing reflection and dialogue to refine ethical judgments.

- Adaptability: Being open to revising decisions as new information and perspectives emerge.

Practical Strategies for Ethical Decision-Making

1. Facilitating Ethical Discussions

Facilitating ethical discussions involves creating a structured and supportive environment for exploring ethical dilemmas. This includes:

- Setting Ground Rules: Establishing ground rules for respectful and open communication.

- Encouraging Participation: Encouraging all parties to share their perspectives and feelings.

- Clarifying Information: Providing clear and accurate information about the medical and ethical aspects of the situation.

2. Documenting Ethical Decisions

Documenting ethical decisions is important for ensuring transparency and accountability. This involves:

- Recording Discussions: Keeping detailed records of ethical discussions and the decision-making process.

- Noting Rationales: Documenting the rationales for decisions made, including the ethical principles and considerations involved.

- Updating Care Plans: Ensuring that care plans are updated to reflect the decisions made and any changes in the patient's preferences or condition.

3. Providing Ethical Education

Providing ethical education to healthcare providers helps enhance their understanding and application of ethical principles. This includes:

- Workshops and Training: Offering workshops and training sessions on ethical decision-making and frameworks.

- Case Studies: Using case studies to illustrate ethical dilemmas and decision-making processes.

- Continuous Learning: Encouraging continuous learning and reflection on ethical practices in healthcare.

Case Studies and Examples

1. Case Study: Informed Consent and Patient Autonomy

A patient is considering a high-risk surgery but is uncertain about the potential outcomes. The chaplain facilitates a discussion with the patient, their family, and the healthcare team. By applying the Four Principles Approach, the chaplain ensures that the patient receives all necessary information (autonomy), the potential benefits and risks are clearly explained (beneficence and non-maleficence), and the patient's decision is respected without pressure (justice).

2. Case Study: Resource Allocation and Justice

During a public health crisis, there is a shortage of ventilators. The healthcare team faces an ethical dilemma about how to allocate limited resources. The chaplain uses the Four Principles Approach to guide the discussion, ensuring that decisions are made based on medical need (beneficence), the least harm is caused (non-maleficence), patient preferences are considered (autonomy), and resources are distributed fairly (justice).

3. Case Study: Confidentiality and Mandatory Reporting

A patient confides in the chaplain about experiencing domestic abuse but fears retaliation if reported. The chaplain faces an ethical dilemma between maintaining confidentiality and the need for mandatory reporting to protect the patient. By applying ethical principles, the chaplain discusses the importance of safety with the patient (beneficence), respects their autonomy by involving them in the decision-making process, and ensures that the necessary steps are taken to protect the patient from harm (non-maleficence and justice).

Ethical decision-making is a critical component of healthcare, requiring a careful balance of principles and practical considerations. Chaplains play a vital role in guiding patients, families, and healthcare providers through ethical dilemmas by using structured frameworks such as the Four Principles Approach. By facilitating ethical discussions, documenting decisions, and providing ethical education, chaplains help ensure that care is compassionate, respectful, and aligned with patients' values and preferences. This chapter has explored various ethical decision-making frameworks, practical strategies for resolving dilemmas, and case studies to illustrate the application of these principles in real-world scenarios. As we continue to prioritize ethical and compassionate care, these practices will remain essential for supporting patients and their families through difficult and complex decisions.

CHAPTER 07

CRISIS INTERVENTION AND TRAUMA SUPPORT

Crisis intervention and trauma support are critical components of a chaplain's role in healthcare settings. Chaplains are often called upon to provide immediate emotional and spiritual support during crisis situations, helping patients, families, and healthcare staff navigate acute distress and trauma. This chapter explores the principles of crisis response, the role of chaplains in crisis intervention, and practical strategies for providing effective support.

Principles of Crisis Response

1. Immediate Presence

The immediate presence of a chaplain during a crisis provides a sense of stability and reassurance. Being physically and emotionally available to those in distress is crucial for effective intervention.

- Availability: Respond promptly to crisis situations, demonstrating a commitment to being there for those in need.

- Visibility: Make your presence known to patients, families, and staff, offering support and comfort.

2. Active Listening

Active listening is essential in crisis intervention. It involves fully engaging with the person in distress, understanding their emotions, and providing empathetic support.

- Empathetic Engagement: Show empathy and understanding by listening without judgment.

- Nonverbal Cues: Use nonverbal cues such as nodding, eye contact, and open body language to convey attentiveness and compassion.

3. Providing Comfort and Reassurance

Offering comfort and reassurance helps individuals feel supported and less isolated during a crisis. Simple gestures and words of encouragement can make a significant difference.

- Verbal Reassurance: Use comforting words and affirmations to provide emotional support.

- Physical Comfort: When appropriate, offer physical comfort through a gentle touch, such as holding a hand or a supportive hug.

4. Facilitating Communication

Effective communication is vital during a crisis. Chaplains help facilitate clear and compassionate communication among patients, families, and healthcare providers.

- Clarifying Information: Ensure that patients and families understand the information provided by healthcare providers.

- Encouraging Expression: Encourage individuals to express their feelings and concerns openly.

5. Mobilizing Resources

Mobilizing additional resources and support is often necessary during a crisis. Chaplains can connect individuals with other professionals and services that can provide further assistance.

- Referrals: Refer patients and families to mental health professionals, social workers, or community support services as needed.

- Support Networks: Help individuals connect with their personal support networks, including family, friends, and spiritual advisors.

The Role of Chaplains in Crisis Intervention

1. Supporting Patients

Patients experiencing a crisis due to sudden illness, trauma, or significant medical events require immediate and compassionate support.

- Emotional Support: Provide a listening ear and empathetic presence to help patients process their emotions.

- Spiritual Support: Offer spiritual guidance, prayer, or rituals that align with the patient's beliefs and provide comfort.

2. Supporting Families

Families often experience significant emotional distress when a loved one is in crisis. Chaplains play a vital role in supporting families through these challenging times.

- Counseling: Provide counseling and support to help families cope with their emotions and make informed decisions.

- Mediation: Facilitate discussions among family members to address concerns and support decision-making.

3. Supporting Healthcare Staff

Healthcare staff may also experience stress and emotional strain during crisis situations. Chaplains offer support to staff, helping them manage their emotions and maintain their well-being.

- Debriefing: Conduct debriefing sessions with healthcare staff to help them process their experiences and emotions.

- Emotional Support: Provide individual or group support sessions to address the emotional needs of staff members.

Practical Strategies for Crisis Intervention

1. Crisis Assessment

Assessing the situation is the first step in crisis intervention. This involves understanding the nature of the crisis, the individuals involved, and their immediate needs.

- Initial Assessment: Quickly assess the situation to determine the severity of the crisis and the needs of those involved.

- Ongoing Monitoring: Continuously monitor the situation and adjust interventions as needed.

2. Stabilization Techniques

Stabilization techniques help individuals regain a sense of control and calm during a crisis. These techniques are essential for immediate support.

- Grounding Exercises: Teach grounding exercises, such as deep breathing or focusing on a specific sensory experience, to help manage acute anxiety.

- Creating a Safe Space: Provide a quiet and safe environment where individuals can express their emotions and feel supported.

3. Providing Information and Guidance

Providing clear and accurate information helps individuals understand the situation and make informed decisions.

- Clarifying Facts: Ensure that individuals have accurate and up-to-date information about the crisis.

- Guidance: Offer guidance on next steps, including available resources and support options.

4. Facilitating Spiritual Practices

Spiritual practices can provide significant comfort and support during a crisis. Chaplains can facilitate these practices to help individuals find peace and strength.

- Prayer and Meditation: Lead or facilitate prayer and meditation sessions that align with the individual's beliefs.

- Rituals and Sacraments: Arrange for religious rituals or sacraments, such as anointing, communion, or last rites, as appropriate.

5. Follow-Up Care

Follow-up care is essential to ensure that individuals continue to receive support after the immediate crisis has passed.

- Check-Ins: Schedule follow-up visits or calls to check on the individual's well-being and provide ongoing support.

- Referrals: Refer individuals to long-term support services, such as counseling or support groups, as needed.

Case Studies and Examples

1. Case Study: Sudden Medical Emergency

A patient experiences a sudden cardiac arrest, and their family is present in the hospital. The chaplain arrives promptly, providing emotional support to the family, listening to their fears and concerns, and offering comforting words. The chaplain facilitates communication between the family and the medical team, ensuring that the family understands the situation. After the immediate crisis, the chaplain follows up with the family to provide ongoing support and resources.

2. Case Study: Traumatic Injury

A young patient is admitted to the emergency room with severe injuries from a car accident. The chaplain supports the patient by staying with them, providing reassurance, and helping them manage their fear and anxiety. The chaplain also supports the patient's parents, offering a calm presence and helping them understand the medical updates. The chaplain arranges for the patient's spiritual advisor to visit and continues to check in with the family throughout the patient's recovery.

3. Case Study: Staff Support After a Critical Incident

Healthcare staff are affected by a critical incident involving a patient's unexpected death. The chaplain conducts a debriefing session with the staff, allowing them to express their emotions and reflect on the experience. The chaplain provides emotional support and offers strategies for coping with stress. Follow-up sessions are arranged to ensure that staff members receive ongoing support and care.

Crisis intervention and trauma support are essential aspects of a chaplain's role in healthcare settings. By providing immediate emotional and spiritual support, facilitating communication, and mobilizing resources, chaplains help patients, families, and healthcare staff navigate acute distress and trauma. This chapter has explored the principles of crisis response, the role of chaplains in crisis intervention, and practical strategies for providing effective support. As we continue to prioritize holistic care, these practices will remain crucial for ensuring that all individuals receive the compassionate and respectful support they need during times of crisis.

TRAUMA- INFORMED CARE

Trauma-informed care is an approach that recognizes the widespread impact of trauma and integrates this understanding into all aspects of care. For chaplains, providing trauma-informed care means being sensitive to the needs of those affected by traumatic events, ensuring that their emotional, psychological, and spiritual needs are addressed with compassion and understanding. This chapter explores the principles of trauma-informed care, the role of chaplains in supporting trauma survivors, and practical strategies for implementing trauma-informed care in healthcare settings.

Understanding Trauma

1. Definition of Trauma

Trauma is an emotional response to a distressing event or series of events that overwhelm an individual's ability to cope. Traumatic events can include but are not limited to, physical or sexual assault, accidents, natural disasters, serious illness, and the sudden loss of a loved one.

- Types of Trauma:

- Acute Trauma: Results from a single incident.

- Chronic Trauma: Results from repeated and prolonged exposure to highly stressful events.

- Complex Trauma: Results from exposure to multiple traumatic events, often of an invasive, interpersonal nature.

2. Impact of Trauma

Trauma can have profound and long-lasting effects on an individual's physical, emotional, and psychological well-being. Common responses to trauma include anxiety, depression, flashbacks, nightmares, and difficulties with trust and relationships.

- Physical Impact: Trauma can lead to chronic pain, fatigue, and other physical symptoms.

- Emotional Impact: Individuals may experience intense emotions such as fear, anger, sadness, and guilt.

- Psychological Impact: Trauma can affect cognitive functions, leading to difficulties with concentration, memory, and decision-making.

Principles of Trauma-Informed Care

1. Safety

Ensuring physical and emotional safety is the first principle of trauma-informed care. Patients and families must feel safe and secure in the healthcare environment.

- Creating a Safe Environment: Make the physical environment comfortable and welcoming.

- Building Trust: Establish trust through consistent and respectful interactions.

2. Trustworthiness and Transparency

Maintaining trustworthiness and transparency in interactions and decision-making processes is crucial for trauma survivors.

- Clear Communication: Provide clear, accurate information about care and treatment.

- Honesty: Be honest about what patients can expect and any uncertainties.

3. Peer Support

Peer support and mutual self-help are important for building trust, establishing safety, and empowering survivors.

- Support Groups: Facilitate access to peer support groups where individuals can share their experiences and support each other.

- Mentorship: Connect patients with peer mentors who have experienced similar challenges.

4. Collaboration and Mutuality

Collaboration and mutuality between patients and healthcare providers are essential for trauma-informed care. This involves recognizing that healing happens in relationships and partnerships.

- Shared Decision-Making: Involve patients in their care decisions, respecting their expertise in their own lives.

- Team Approach: Work collaboratively with other healthcare providers to ensure holistic care.

5. Empowerment, Voice, and Choice

Empowering patients by providing them with choices and control over their care helps to rebuild a sense of agency and self-efficacy.

- Empowering Language: Use language that empowers patients, avoiding medical jargon and condescending tones.

- Supporting Autonomy: Respect patients' choices and preferences in their care.

6. Cultural, Historical, and Gender Issues

Recognizing and addressing cultural, historical, and gender issues is essential for providing trauma-informed care that respects and honors each patient's unique background and experiences.

- Cultural Competence: Be aware of and sensitive to cultural differences in responses to trauma and healing practices.

- Gender Sensitivity: Recognize the impact of gender on trauma experiences and recovery.

The Role of Chaplains in Trauma-Informed Care

1. Providing Emotional and Spiritual Support

Chaplains provide critical emotional and spiritual support to trauma survivors, helping them process their experiences and find meaning and hope.

- Active Listening: Offer a compassionate, nonjudgmental presence and listen to patients' stories.

- Spiritual Counseling: Provide spiritual counseling and guidance tailored to the patient's beliefs and needs.

2. Facilitating Healing Practices

Chaplains facilitate healing practices that can help trauma survivors cope with their experiences and promote recovery.

- Prayer and Meditation: Lead or facilitate prayer and meditation sessions that offer comfort and peace.

- Rituals and Ceremonies: Arrange for religious rituals or ceremonies that provide a sense of closure and healing.

3. Advocating for Trauma-Informed Practices

Chaplains advocate for trauma-informed practices within the healthcare team, ensuring that all aspects of care are sensitive to the needs of trauma survivors.

- Education and Training: Educate healthcare providers about the principles of trauma-informed care and the impact of trauma on patients.

- Policy Development: Advocate for policies and practices that support trauma-informed care in the healthcare setting.

Practical Strategies for Implementing Trauma-Informed Care

1. Conducting Trauma Assessments

Assessing the impact of trauma on patients is the first step in providing trauma-informed care. This involves:

- Trauma Screening: Use trauma screening tools to identify patients who may have experienced trauma.

- Comprehensive Assessment: Conduct a comprehensive assessment to understand the nature and impact of the trauma on the patient's well-being.

2. Creating a Safe and Supportive Environment

Creating a safe and supportive environment is crucial for trauma survivors. This involves:

- Physical Environment: Ensure that the physical environment is safe, comfortable, and welcoming.

- Emotional Safety: Foster an atmosphere of trust and respect where patients feel emotionally safe.

3. Building Trust and Rapport

Building trust and rapport with trauma survivors is essential for effective care. This involves:

- Consistent Support: Provide consistent and reliable support to build trust over time.

- Transparent Communication: Communicate openly and honestly, keeping patients informed about their care.

4. Encouraging Empowerment and Participation

Empowering patients to participate in their care helps to restore a sense of control and agency. This involves:

- Informed Consent: Ensure that patients are fully informed about their treatment options and involve them in decision-making.

- Choice and Control: Provide patients with choices and support their autonomy in making care decisions.

5. Utilizing Trauma-Informed Interventions

Utilize interventions that are sensitive to the needs of trauma survivors and promote healing. This involves:

- Grounding Techniques: Teach grounding techniques, such as deep breathing and mindfulness, to help manage distress.

- Therapeutic Approaches: Use therapeutic approaches, such as cognitive-behavioral therapy or narrative therapy, that are effective in addressing trauma.

Case Studies and Examples

1. Case Study: Supporting a Patient with a History of Abuse

A patient with a history of domestic abuse is admitted to the hospital for surgery. The chaplain conducts a trauma assessment and learns about the patient's background. The chaplain provides emotional support, offers grounding techniques to manage anxiety, and arranges for a private room to ensure the patient's safety and comfort. The chaplain also facilitates access to a support group for survivors of abuse.

2. Case Study: Trauma-Informed Care for a Pediatric Patient

A child who has experienced a traumatic accident is receiving care in the hospital. The chaplain works with the healthcare team to create a safe and supportive environment, involving the child's family in the care plan. The chaplain uses play therapy to help the child express their emotions and coordinates with a child psychologist for additional support. The chaplain also provides spiritual care to the family, helping them navigate their emotional responses.

3. Case Study: Addressing Historical Trauma

An Indigenous patient is experiencing health issues related to historical trauma. The chaplain recognizes the impact of historical and cultural factors on the patient's well-being. The chaplain facilitates a healing ceremony led by an Indigenous spiritual leader and advocates for culturally appropriate care within the healthcare team. The chaplain also educates the team about the patient's cultural background and the importance of cultural sensitivity in their care.

Understanding the impact of trauma and providing trauma-informed care are essential components of a chaplain's role in healthcare settings. By recognizing the principles of trauma-informed care, providing emotional and spiritual support, and implementing practical strategies, chaplains can ensure that the needs of trauma survivors are addressed with compassion and sensitivity. This chapter has explored the principles of trauma-informed care, the role of chaplains in supporting trauma survivors, and practical strategies for implementing trauma-informed care. As we continue to prioritize holistic and compassionate care, these practices will remain crucial for supporting individuals affected by trauma and promoting their healing and recovery.

CHAPTER 08

END-OF-LIFE CARE AND BEREAVEMENT SUPPORT

End-of-life care is a sensitive and crucial aspect of healthcare, focusing on providing comfort, dignity, and support to patients nearing the end of their lives and their families. Chaplains play a vital role in offering spiritual guidance and bereavement support, helping individuals navigate the emotional and spiritual complexities of this challenging time. This chapter explores the principles of end-of-life care, the role of chaplains in supporting patients and families, and practical strategies for providing effective bereavement support.

Principles of End-of-Life Care

1. Comfort and Symptom Management

The primary goal of end-of-life care is to ensure that patients are as comfortable as possible, managing symptoms such as pain, shortness of breath, and anxiety.

- Pain Management: Collaborate with medical staff to ensure effective pain relief.

- Symptom Control: Address other symptoms, such as nausea, fatigue, and difficulty breathing, to enhance comfort.

2. Dignity and Respect

Maintaining the dignity and respect of patients is essential. This involves honoring their preferences, values, and cultural beliefs.

- Personalized Care: Provide care that is tailored to the individual's needs and preferences.

- Respect for Wishes: Ensure that the patient's end-of-life wishes, including advance directives, are respected and followed.

3. Emotional and Spiritual Support

Providing emotional and spiritual support is crucial for both patients and their families during end-of-life care.

- Emotional Support: Offer a compassionate presence, listening to and validating the emotions of patients and families.

- Spiritual Support: Provide spiritual guidance, prayer, and rituals that align with the patient's beliefs and offer comfort.

4. Family Involvement

Involving the family in the care process is important for providing holistic support and ensuring that the patient's loved ones feel included and supported.

- Open Communication: Maintain open lines of communication with the family, keeping them informed and involved in care decisions.

- Support for Caregivers: Offer support and resources to family members who are acting as caregivers.

The Role of Chaplains in End-of-Life Care

1. Providing Spiritual Guidance

Chaplains offer spiritual guidance to patients and families, helping them find meaning, hope, and peace during the end-of-life journey.

- Spiritual Counseling: Engage in conversations about spiritual beliefs, fears, and hopes.

- Rituals and Sacraments: Facilitate religious rituals and sacraments, such as communion, anointing, or last rites.

2. Facilitating Communication

Chaplains help facilitate communication between patients, families, and healthcare providers, ensuring that everyone is on the same page and that the patient's wishes are respected.

- Advance Directives: Assist in discussing and documenting advance directives and end-of-life wishes.

- Conflict Resolution: Mediate any conflicts or misunderstandings that may arise among family members or between the family and healthcare team.

3. Offering Bereavement Support

Bereavement support is a critical aspect of a chaplain's role, helping families cope with the loss of a loved one and navigate the grieving process.

- Grief Counseling: Provide counseling to help individuals process their grief and find healthy ways to cope.

- Memorial Services: Facilitate or conduct memorial services and funerals that honor the deceased and provide closure for the family.

4. Supporting Healthcare Staff

Healthcare staff can also experience emotional and spiritual challenges when providing end-of-life care. Chaplains offer support to staff to help them manage their feelings and maintain their well-being.

- Debriefing Sessions: Conduct debriefing sessions with staff after the death of a patient to provide emotional support and reflection.

- Ongoing Support: Offer ongoing support and resources to staff members coping with the emotional demands of end-of-life care.

Practical Strategies for End-of-Life Care

1. Conducting Comprehensive Assessments

A comprehensive assessment helps identify the physical, emotional, and spiritual needs of the patient and their family.

- Holistic Assessment: Assess the patient's physical symptoms, emotional state, and spiritual needs.

- Family Needs: Evaluate the needs and concerns of the family to provide appropriate support.

2. Creating a Comforting Environment

Creating a peaceful and comforting environment can significantly enhance the quality of end-of-life care.

- Personal Touches: Incorporate personal items, music, or other comforting elements into the patient's room.

- Quiet Space: Ensure that the environment is quiet and conducive to rest and reflection.

3. Implementing Palliative Care Practices

Palliative care focuses on providing relief from symptoms and improving the quality of life for patients with serious illnesses.

- Pain Management Protocols: Work with the healthcare team to implement effective pain management protocols.

- Symptom Relief: Address other distressing symptoms with appropriate interventions.

4. Encouraging Open Communication

Encouraging open and honest communication among patients, families, and healthcare providers is essential for effective end-of-life care.

- Regular Updates: Provide regular updates to the family about the patient's condition and care plan.

- Facilitated Conversations: Facilitate conversations about end-of-life wishes, fears, and concerns.

5. Providing Spiritual and Emotional Support

Offering consistent spiritual and emotional support helps patients and families feel cared for and understood.

- Regular Visits: Make regular visits to the patient and family to offer ongoing support.

- Spiritual Resources: Provide spiritual resources, such as religious texts, prayer books, and meditation guides.

Bereavement Support Strategies

1. Immediate Support After Death

Providing immediate support to the family after the death of a loved one is crucial for helping them navigate the initial stages of grief.

- Presence and Compassion: Be present with the family, offering compassion and a listening ear.

- Practical Assistance: Assist with practical tasks, such as contacting a funeral home or making arrangements for a memorial service.

2. Facilitating Grief Counseling

Grief counseling helps individuals process their emotions and find ways to cope with their loss.

- One-on-One Counseling: Offer individual counseling sessions to address personal grief experiences.

- Support Groups: Facilitate or refer individuals to support groups where they can share their experiences with others who have experienced similar losses.

3. Conducting Memorial Services

Memorial services provide an opportunity for families to honor their loved ones and find closure.

- Personalized Services: Conduct or facilitate personalized memorial services that reflect the values and wishes of the deceased and their family.

- Cultural Sensitivity: Ensure that the memorial service respects and incorporates the cultural and religious traditions of the family.

4. Offering Long-Term Support

Bereavement support should continue beyond the immediate aftermath of the death, as grief can be a long-term process.

- Follow-Up Visits: Schedule follow-up visits or calls to check on the family's well-being and provide ongoing support.

- Resources and Referrals: Provide resources, such as books and articles on grief, and refer individuals to professional grief counselors or therapists if needed.

Case Studies and Examples

1. Case Study: Supporting a Terminally Ill Patient

A patient with terminal cancer expresses a desire for spiritual support as they approach the end of life. The chaplain conducts regular visits, providing spiritual counseling and facilitating conversations about the patient's fears and hopes. The chaplain also arranges for the patient to receive the sacraments of their faith and supports the family through the process. After the patient's death, the chaplain continues to provide bereavement support to the family, helping them navigate their grief.

2. Case Study: Bereavement Support for a Sudden Loss

A family experiences the sudden loss of a loved one due to a heart attack. The chaplain provides immediate support by staying with the family, listening to their emotions, and offering words of comfort. The chaplain assists with practical arrangements for the funeral and conducts the memorial service. In the following months, the chaplain continues to check in with the family, providing grief counseling and connecting them with a support group.

3. Case Study: End-of-Life Care for a Child

A child with a life-limiting illness is receiving end-of-life care in the hospital. The chaplain works with the healthcare team to ensure that the child's symptoms are managed and that their wishes are respected. The chaplain provides emotional and spiritual support to the child's parents, helping them cope with their emotions and make difficult decisions. After the child's death, the chaplain facilitates a memorial service and offers ongoing bereavement support to the family.

End-of-life care and bereavement support are essential aspects of a chaplain's role in healthcare settings. By providing comfort, dignity, and support to patients and their families, chaplains help navigate the emotional and spiritual complexities of the end-of-life journey. This chapter has explored the principles of end-of-life care, the role of chaplains in supporting patients and families, and practical strategies for providing effective bereavement support. As we continue to prioritize compassionate and holistic care, these practices will remain crucial for ensuring that all individuals receive the support and respect they deserve during this profound time of transition.

RITUALS AND PRACTICES

Religious rituals and practices play a significant role in providing comfort, meaning, and a sense of continuity to patients and families during end-of-life care. Chaplains facilitate these practices, ensuring that the spiritual and cultural needs of individuals are respected and honored. This chapter explores the importance of rituals and practices in end-of-life care, the role of chaplains in facilitating these rituals, and practical strategies for incorporating them into care.

The Importance of Rituals and Practices

1. Providing Comfort and Reassurance

Religious rituals and practices offer comfort and reassurance to patients and families during end-of-life care by connecting them to their faith and traditions.

- Spiritual Comfort: Rituals provide a sense of spiritual comfort and peace, helping individuals feel supported by their faith.

- Familiarity: The familiarity of rituals can be soothing, offering a sense of continuity and normalcy during a time of uncertainty.

2. Creating Meaning and Purpose

Rituals and practices help individuals find meaning and purpose in their experiences, offering a framework to understand and cope with the end of life.

- Meaning-Making: Rituals help individuals make sense of their experiences and find meaning in the midst of suffering and loss.

- Legacy: Rituals can honor the life and legacy of the dying person, celebrating their contributions and impact.

3. Fostering Connection and Community

Rituals and practices foster a sense of connection and community, bringing together family, friends, and faith communities to support the patient and each other.

- Shared Experience: Rituals provide a shared experience that strengthens bonds and offers mutual support.

- Community Support: Involving the faith community in rituals can provide additional support and resources for patients and families.

The Role of Chaplains in Facilitating Rituals and Practices

1. Understanding Diverse Religious Traditions

Chaplains must have a broad understanding of various religious traditions and practices to effectively facilitate rituals that are meaningful to patients and families.

- Religious Literacy: Develop knowledge of the beliefs, rituals, and practices of different faith traditions.

- Cultural Sensitivity: Respect and honor the cultural and religious diversity of patients and families.

2. Assessing Spiritual Needs and Preferences

Conducting a spiritual assessment helps chaplains identify the specific rituals and practices that are important to the patient and their family.

- Open-Ended Questions: Ask open-ended questions to explore the patient's spiritual needs and preferences. For example, "Are there any religious or spiritual practices that are important to you at this time?"

- Listening: Listen attentively to understand the significance of specific rituals and practices for the patient and family.

3. Facilitating Rituals and Practices

Chaplains play a crucial role in facilitating religious rituals and practices, ensuring they are conducted in a way that is meaningful and respectful.

- Coordination: Coordinate with religious leaders, family members, and healthcare providers to facilitate rituals.

- Adaptation: Adapt rituals as needed to accommodate the hospital setting and the patient's condition.

4. Providing Spiritual Resources

Chaplains can provide spiritual resources, such as religious texts, prayer books, and ritual items, to support the practice of rituals.

- Resource Availability: Ensure that spiritual resources are readily available for patients and families.

- Access to Clergy: Facilitate access to clergy or religious leaders who can perform specific rituals or provide additional support.

Practical Strategies for Incorporating Rituals into End-of-Life Care

1. Creating a Sacred Space

Creating a sacred space in the patient's room or within the hospital can enhance the experience of religious rituals and practices.

- Quiet and Privacy: Ensure that the space is quiet and offers privacy for the patient and family.

- Personal Touches: Incorporate personal and religious items, such as candles, prayer rugs, or icons, to create a sacred atmosphere.

2. Facilitating Common Religious Rituals

Understanding and facilitating common religious rituals can provide comfort and support to patients and families. Examples include:

- Christian Rituals: Administering sacraments such as communion, anointing of the sick, or last rites.

- Jewish Rituals: Facilitating prayers, reciting the Shema, or coordinating with a rabbi for specific rituals.

- Muslim Rituals: Ensuring that the patient can perform daily prayers, providing access to the Quran, and coordinating with an imam for specific needs.

- Hindu Rituals: Arranging for the recitation of sacred texts, facilitating rituals such as puja, and providing access to a Hindu priest.

- Buddhist Rituals: Facilitating meditation sessions, providing access to Buddhist texts, and coordinating with a Buddhist monk for specific practices.

3. Involving Family and Community

Involving family and the patient's faith community in rituals can provide additional support and enhance the significance of the practices.

- Family Participation: Encourage family members to participate in rituals, offering them a sense of involvement and support.

- Community Support: Coordinate with the patient's faith community to provide additional resources and support.

4. Adapting Rituals for the Healthcare Setting

Adapting rituals to fit the healthcare setting ensures that they can be performed in a way that is meaningful and respectful, despite any limitations.

- Flexibility: Be flexible and creative in adapting rituals to accommodate the patient's condition and the hospital environment.

- Collaboration: Work with healthcare providers to ensure that rituals do not interfere with medical care and that they are conducted safely.

Case Studies and Examples

1. Case Study: Administering Last Rites

A Catholic patient is nearing the end of life and requests the sacrament of last rites. The chaplain coordinates with a priest to administer the sacrament, ensuring that the family is present and involved in the ritual. The chaplain also provides a quiet and private space for the sacrament to be performed, offering additional prayers and support to the family.

2. Case Study: Facilitating a Hindu Ritual

A Hindu patient expresses a desire to perform a final puja (worship ritual) before passing. The chaplain arranges for the necessary ritual items, including incense, flowers, and a small idol. The chaplain coordinates with the patient's family and a Hindu priest to facilitate the ritual in the patient's room, ensuring that the patient's spiritual needs are honored and respected.

3. Case Study: Supporting a Buddhist Meditation Practice

A Buddhist patient nearing the end of life finds comfort in meditation. The chaplain provides a quiet space and arranges for a Buddhist monk to visit and lead meditation sessions. The chaplain also provides access to Buddhist texts and offers additional spiritual support to the patient and family.

4. Case Study: Jewish End-of-Life Prayers

A Jewish patient nearing the end of life requests the recitation of the Shema and other prayers. The chaplain coordinates with a rabbi to visit the patient and lead the prayers. The chaplain also provides a prayer book and facilitates the presence of family members, ensuring that the patient's spiritual needs are met.

Conclusion

Religious rituals and practices are integral to providing comfort, meaning, and support to patients and families during end-of-life care. Chaplains play a vital role in facilitating these rituals, ensuring that the spiritual and cultural needs of individuals are respected and honored. This chapter has explored the importance of rituals and practices in end-of-life care, the role of chaplains in facilitating these rituals, and practical strategies for incorporating them into care. As we continue to prioritize holistic and compassionate care, these practices will remain crucial for ensuring that all individuals receive the spiritual support and respect they deserve during this profound time of transition.

CHAPTER 09

SELF-CARE FOR CHAPLAINS

Self-care is essential for chaplains to maintain their well-being, resilience, and effectiveness in providing spiritual and emotional support to others. The demanding nature of chaplaincy work, particularly in healthcare settings, requires intentional self-care practices to prevent burnout and compassion fatigue. This chapter explores the importance of self-care for chaplains, various self-care practices, and strategies for integrating self-care into daily routines.

The Importance of Self-Care

1. Preventing Burnout and Compassion Fatigue

Chaplains often encounter high levels of stress and emotional exhaustion due to their continuous exposure to suffering and trauma. Without adequate self-care, chaplains are at risk of burnout and compassion fatigue, which can impair their ability to provide effective care.

- Burnout: A state of physical, emotional, and mental exhaustion caused by prolonged stress and overwork.

- Compassion Fatigue: The emotional strain of exposure to working with those suffering from the consequences of traumatic events.

2. Enhancing Personal Well-Being

Self-care promotes overall well-being, helping chaplains maintain a healthy balance in their lives. This includes physical health, emotional stability, and spiritual vitality.

- Physical Well-Being: Maintaining physical health through exercise, nutrition, and rest.

- Emotional Well-Being: Managing stress and emotions through healthy coping mechanisms.

- Spiritual Well-Being: Nurturing one's own spiritual life and maintaining a connection with one's faith and values.

3. Ensuring Effectiveness in Care

Effective self-care enables chaplains to be more present, empathetic, and effective in their work. By taking care of themselves, chaplains can better support their patients and families.

- Enhanced Empathy: Being emotionally available and empathetic towards others.

- Sustained Energy: Having the physical and emotional energy to meet the demands of chaplaincy work.

- Professional Growth: Continuously developing and maintaining professional skills and knowledge.

Physical Self-Care Practices

1. Regular Exercise

Regular physical activity is essential for maintaining physical health and reducing stress. Exercise can improve mood, increase energy levels, and promote better sleep.

- Daily Routine: Incorporate exercise into your daily routine, such as walking, jogging, yoga, or other physical activities you enjoy.

- Consistency: Aim for consistency rather than intensity; even moderate exercise can have significant benefits.

2. Healthy Nutrition

A balanced diet is crucial for maintaining physical health and energy levels. Proper nutrition can also enhance mood and cognitive function.

- Balanced Diet: Eat a variety of foods that provide essential nutrients, including fruits, vegetables, whole grains, lean proteins, and healthy fats.

- Hydration: Stay hydrated by drinking plenty of water throughout the day.

3. Adequate Rest and Sleep

Rest and sleep are vital for physical and emotional recovery. Adequate sleep helps improve concentration, mood, and overall well-being.

- Sleep Hygiene: Maintain a regular sleep schedule and create a restful sleep environment.

- Rest Breaks: Take short breaks during the day to rest and recharge.

Emotional Self-Care Practices

1. Stress Management

Effective stress management techniques are essential for emotional well-being. These techniques can help reduce anxiety, improve focus, and promote relaxation.

- Mindfulness and Meditation: Practice mindfulness and meditation to stay present and manage stress.

- Relaxation Techniques: Use relaxation techniques such as deep breathing, progressive muscle relaxation, or visualization.

2. Emotional Expression

Expressing emotions in healthy ways is crucial for emotional well-being. This can include talking with trusted individuals, journaling, or creative outlets.

- Support Systems: Maintain strong support systems, including family, friends, and colleagues, with whom you can share your feelings and experiences.

- Professional Support: Consider seeking professional support, such as counseling or therapy, to process emotions and stress.

3. Setting Boundaries

Setting boundaries is important for protecting your emotional health and preventing burnout. This includes managing workload and ensuring time for self-care.

- Work-Life Balance: Strive for a balance between work and personal life, ensuring time for relaxation and activities you enjoy.

- Saying No: Learn to say no to additional responsibilities when you are already feeling overwhelmed.

Spiritual Self-Care Practices

1. Personal Spiritual Practices

Nurturing your own spiritual life is essential for maintaining spiritual well-being. Engage in practices that connect you with your faith and values.

- Prayer and Meditation: Set aside time each day for prayer or meditation to reflect and find peace.

- Sacred Texts: Read and reflect on sacred texts or spiritual literature that inspire and comfort you.

2. Participation in Faith Community

Being part of a faith community provides spiritual support and a sense of belonging. Participate in community activities and worship services.

- Regular Worship: Attend regular worship services or spiritual gatherings that align with your beliefs.

- Community Involvement: Engage in community activities, such as study groups, volunteer work, or social events, to build connections and support.

3. Reflection and Renewal

Regular reflection and spiritual renewal help maintain a sense of purpose and meaning in your work. Set aside time for retreats or spiritual reflection.

- Spiritual Retreats: Participate in spiritual retreats or quiet days for reflection and renewal.

- Reflective Practices: Engage in reflective practices, such as journaling or contemplative walks, to deepen your spiritual awareness.

Strategies for Integrating Self-Care into Daily Routine

1. Creating a Self-Care Plan

Developing a personalized self-care plan can help you integrate self-care practices into your daily routine. Identify activities that nurture your physical, emotional, and spiritual well-being.

- Personal Assessment: Assess your current self-care practices and identify areas for improvement.

- Goal Setting: Set realistic and achievable self-care goals that align with your needs and preferences.

- Action Plan: Create a detailed action plan that outlines specific self-care activities and how you will incorporate them into your routine.

2. Prioritizing Self-Care

Prioritizing self-care means making it a non-negotiable part of your daily life. Recognize that self-care is essential for your well-being and effectiveness as a chaplain.

- Scheduled Time: Schedule dedicated time for self-care activities in your calendar.

- Daily Practice: Make self-care a daily practice, even if it's just a few minutes each day.

3. Seeking Support and Accountability

Having support and accountability can help you stay committed to your self-care plan. Share your self-care goals with trusted individuals who can encourage and support you.

- Support Networks: Connect with colleagues, friends, or family members who can provide support and accountability.

- Professional Support: Consider joining a professional group or seeking mentorship to support your self-care efforts.

Case Studies and Examples

1. Case Study: Establishing a Routine for Physical Health

A chaplain recognizes the need to improve their physical health and decides to establish a routine that includes daily walks and a balanced diet. They set a goal to walk for 30 minutes each morning and plan meals that include a variety of nutritious foods. By prioritizing physical health, the chaplain experiences increased energy and a better mood, which enhances their ability to support patients and families.

2. Case Study: Managing Stress Through Mindfulness

A chaplain experiences high levels of stress due to the emotional demands of their work. They decide to incorporate mindfulness practices into their daily routine, setting aside 10 minutes each morning for meditation. Over time, the chaplain notices a reduction in stress and an increased ability to remain present and empathetic with patients.

3. Case Study: Spiritual Renewal Through Retreats

A chaplain feels spiritually drained and decides to attend a weekend spiritual retreat. The retreat provides time for prayer, reflection, and connection with other spiritual leaders. The chaplain returns feeling renewed and recommitted to their work, with a deeper sense of purpose and connection to their faith.

Self-care is crucial for chaplains to maintain their well-being, resilience, and effectiveness in providing spiritual and emotional support to others. By prioritizing physical, emotional, and spiritual self-care practices, chaplains can prevent burnout, enhance their personal well-being, and ensure that they are able to offer compassionate and effective care. This chapter has explored the importance of self-care for chaplains, various self-care practices, and strategies for integrating self-care into daily routines. As we continue to prioritize holistic and compassionate care, these self-care practices will remain essential for sustaining the well-being and effectiveness of chaplains in their vital work.

STRATEGIES FOR SELF-CARE

Chaplains face unique challenges and stressors in their roles, making self-care essential for maintaining their well-being and effectiveness. Implementing strategic self-care practices helps chaplains manage stress, avoid burnout, and sustain their ability to provide compassionate care. This chapter explores key strategies for self-care, including regular reflection, supervision, peer support, and maintaining a healthy work-life balance.

Regular Reflection

1. Importance of Reflection

Regular reflection allows chaplains to process their experiences, gain insights, and maintain emotional and spiritual health. Reflection helps chaplains stay grounded and connected to their purpose and values.

- Self-Awareness: Enhances self-awareness and understanding of personal reactions and feelings.

- Emotional Processing: Provides a space to process emotions and experiences, reducing stress and emotional overload.

2. Reflective Practices

Incorporating reflective practices into daily routines can support ongoing self-care and personal growth.

- Journaling: Writing about daily experiences, thoughts, and feelings can provide clarity and emotional release.

- Meditation: Practicing meditation or mindfulness helps chaplains stay present and manage stress.

- Prayer and Contemplation: Engaging in prayer or contemplative practices supports spiritual well-being and connection to faith.

3. Structured Reflection

Structured reflection involves setting aside specific times for in-depth reflection on experiences and challenges.

- Regular Reflection Sessions: Schedule regular reflection sessions, such as weekly or monthly, to review experiences and insights.

- Guided Reflection: Use guided reflection questions or frameworks to deepen the reflective process.

Supervision

1. Role of Supervision

Supervision provides a supportive space for chaplains to discuss their work, receive feedback, and gain new perspectives. Supervision helps chaplains address challenges, enhance skills, and maintain professional boundaries.

- Professional Growth: Supports ongoing professional development and skill enhancement.

- Emotional Support: Offers a safe space to discuss emotional challenges and receive support.

2. Types of Supervision

Different types of supervision can provide diverse benefits and support.

- Individual Supervision: One-on-one sessions with a supervisor to discuss personal and professional challenges.

- Group Supervision: Group sessions with peers to share experiences, insights, and support.

- Peer Supervision: Peer-to-peer supervision involves colleagues supporting each other through discussion and feedback.

3. Implementing Supervision

To effectively implement supervision, chaplains should seek regular opportunities and engage actively in the process.

- Finding a Supervisor: Identify a qualified supervisor with experience in chaplaincy or a related field.

- Regular Sessions: Schedule regular supervision sessions, such as bi-weekly or monthly.

- Active Participation: Engage actively in supervision, sharing experiences, and being open to feedback and guidance.

Peer Support

1. Importance of Peer Support

Peer support provides a sense of community and shared understanding among chaplains. Connecting with peers helps chaplains feel less isolated and more supported.

- Shared Experiences: Allows chaplains to share experiences and challenges with others who understand their role.

- Emotional Support: Provides emotional support and encouragement from colleagues.

2. Building Peer Support Networks

Building and maintaining peer support networks can enhance chaplains' well-being and professional satisfaction.

- Regular Meetings: Organize regular meetings or informal gatherings with peers to share experiences and support.

- Online Communities: Participate in online communities or forums for chaplains to connect and support each other.

- Mentorship Programs: Engage in mentorship programs where experienced chaplains mentor newer colleagues.

3. Effective Peer Support Practices

Effective peer support practices involve active listening, empathy, and mutual respect.

- Active Listening: Listen actively and empathetically to peers' experiences and concerns.

- Encouragement: Offer encouragement and positive feedback to support peers' well-being.

- Resource Sharing: Share resources, ideas, and strategies for self-care and professional growth.

Maintaining a Healthy Work-Life Balance

1. Importance of Work-Life Balance

Maintaining a healthy work-life balance is essential for preventing burnout and sustaining overall well-being. Balancing work responsibilities with personal life allows chaplains to recharge and maintain their health.

- Prevents Burnout: Helps prevent burnout by ensuring time for rest and personal activities.

- Enhances Well-Being: Supports physical, emotional, and spiritual well-being.

2. Strategies for Work-Life Balance

Implementing strategies to maintain a healthy work-life balance can support long-term well-being and effectiveness.

- Setting Boundaries: Set clear boundaries between work and personal life, such as specific work hours and time off.

- Time Management: Use effective time management techniques to prioritize tasks and reduce stress.

- Delegation: Delegate tasks when possible to manage workload and prevent overwork.

3. Prioritizing Personal Activities

Prioritizing personal activities and interests outside of work is crucial for maintaining balance and well-being.

- Hobbies and Interests: Engage in hobbies and activities that bring joy and relaxation.

- Quality Time: Spend quality time with family and friends to strengthen personal relationships.

- Self-Care Activities: Incorporate self-care activities, such as exercise, relaxation, and leisure, into daily routines.

Case Studies and Examples

1. Case Study: Integrating Reflection into Daily Routine

A chaplain incorporates daily journaling and weekly meditation sessions into their routine. This practice helps them process their experiences, manage stress, and maintain a strong connection to their spiritual life. The chaplain notices improved emotional well-being and a greater ability to support patients effectively.

2. Case Study: Utilizing Supervision for Professional Growth

A chaplain schedules regular bi-weekly supervision sessions with a seasoned supervisor. During these sessions, the chaplain discusses challenging cases, receives feedback, and explores new strategies for providing care. The supervision helps the chaplain develop professionally and maintain emotional resilience.

3. Case Study: Building a Peer Support Network

A group of chaplains organizes monthly peer support meetings where they share experiences, offer support, and discuss self-care strategies. These meetings provide a valuable sense of community and mutual support, helping each chaplain feel less isolated and more empowered in their role.

4. Case Study: Achieving Work-Life Balance

A chaplain sets clear boundaries between work and personal life, ensuring that evenings and weekends are reserved for family time and personal activities. The chaplain also practices time management techniques to prioritize tasks and avoid overwork. As a result, the chaplain experiences improved well-being and a better ability to engage fully in both work and personal life.

Self-care is essential for chaplains to maintain their well-being, resilience, and effectiveness in their roles. By implementing strategies such as regular reflection, supervision, peer support, and maintaining a healthy work-life balance, chaplains can prevent burnout, enhance their personal well-being, and sustain their ability to provide compassionate care. This chapter has explored the importance of self-care, various self-care practices, and practical strategies for integrating self-care into daily routines. As we continue to prioritize holistic and compassionate care, these self-care practices will remain crucial for sustaining the well-being and effectiveness of chaplains in their vital work.

CHAPTER 10

CASE STUDIES

Case studies provide practical, real-life examples of the challenges and successes chaplains may encounter in their work. These scenarios illustrate the application of the concepts discussed throughout this book, offering insights into how chaplains can effectively provide spiritual care, support patients and families, navigate ethical dilemmas, and practice self-care. Each case study is followed by an analysis to highlight key learnings and best practices.

Case Study 1: Supporting a Terminally Ill Patient

Scenario:

John, a 68-year-old man diagnosed with terminal cancer, is admitted to the hospital. He is experiencing severe pain and emotional distress as he comes to terms with his prognosis. John is a devout Christian and finds comfort in his faith. His family is also deeply religious and involved in his care.

Intervention:

The chaplain conducts a spiritual assessment, discovering that John finds solace in prayer and reading the Bible. The chaplain visits John daily, offering spiritual counseling and prayer. They arrange for John to receive communion and involve his family in the sessions. The chaplain also coordinates with the medical team to ensure John's pain is managed effectively.

Outcome:

John reports feeling more at peace and less anxious. His family feels supported and involved in his care. The coordinated efforts of the chaplain and medical team ensure that John's physical, emotional, and spiritual needs are met.

Analysis:

- Spiritual Assessment: Understanding John's faith and incorporating it into his care provided significant comfort.

- Family Involvement: Involving the family strengthened their support system and helped them cope with the situation.

- Holistic Care: Addressing physical pain, emotional distress, and spiritual needs holistically improved John's overall well-being.

Case Study 2: Navigating an Ethical Dilemma

Scenario:

Maria, a 45-year-old woman, is in a coma following a severe stroke. Her family is divided on whether to continue life-sustaining treatment. Maria's husband wants to withdraw treatment based on her previously expressed wishes, while her parents want to continue all possible interventions.

Intervention:

The chaplain facilitates a family meeting, creating a safe space for open discussion. They listen to each family member's perspective, acknowledging their emotions and concerns. The chaplain helps clarify Maria's advance directive and explains the ethical principles of autonomy and beneficence. They also involve the healthcare team to provide medical insights and potential outcomes.

Outcome:

Through guided discussions, the family reaches a consensus to honor Maria's wishes and transition to palliative care. The chaplain continues to support the family emotionally and spiritually during this difficult decision.

Analysis:

- Facilitating Communication: Creating a space for open discussion helped the family navigate their conflicting views.

- Ethical Guidance: Explaining ethical principles and Maria's advance directive provided clarity and direction.

- Emotional Support: Ongoing support helped the family cope with their decision and the grieving process.

Case Study 3: Providing Crisis Intervention

Scenario:

A hospital experiences a sudden influx of patients due to a natural disaster. Among them is a young mother, Lisa, who is critically injured. Her husband and two children are in the waiting area, overwhelmed with fear and uncertainty.

Intervention:

The chaplain immediately offers emotional support to Lisa's family, providing a calm and reassuring presence. They ensure the family receives regular updates from the medical team and facilitate communication. The chaplain also engages the children in age-appropriate activities to help distract them from the stress.

Outcome:

Lisa's family feels supported and less anxious despite the chaotic situation. The children are calmer, and the husband appreciates the chaplain's guidance and support. Lisa receives the critical care she needs while her family is well cared for.

Analysis:

- Immediate Presence: Being present and providing immediate support was crucial in managing the family's anxiety.

-        Effective   Communication: Facilitating communication between the medical team and the family ensured they were informed and reassured.

- Age-Appropriate Support: Addressing the children's needs helped reduce their stress and provided a sense of normalcy.

Case Study 4: Facilitating a Religious Ritual

Scenario:

Ravi, a 75-year-old Hindu patient, is in the final stages of life. He expresses a strong desire to perform a final puja (worship ritual) with his family before passing. The hospital staff is unfamiliar with Hindu rituals and looks to the chaplain for guidance.

Intervention:

The chaplain coordinates with Ravi's family to understand the specific requirements for the puja. They arrange for the necessary ritual items, including flowers, incense, and a small idol. The chaplain ensures that Ravi's room is set up to create a sacred space and allows the family privacy during the ritual. They also arrange for a Hindu priest to perform the puja.

Outcome:

Ravi and his family are deeply appreciative of the effort to honor their religious practices. The puja provides Ravi with spiritual comfort and a sense of peace. The family finds solace in fulfilling Ravi's wishes and feels supported by the hospital staff.

Analysis:

- Cultural Sensitivity: Understanding and respecting Ravi's religious needs ensured his spiritual well-being.

- Coordination: Effective coordination with the family and healthcare team facilitated a meaningful ritual.

- Creating Sacred Space: Adapting the hospital environment to accommodate the ritual provided a sense of comfort and respect.

Case Study 5: Supporting Healthcare Staff

Scenario:

A beloved nurse, Sarah, suddenly passes away due to a car accident, deeply affecting the hospital staff. The team is struggling with grief and shock, impacting their ability to provide care.

Intervention:

The chaplain organizes a debriefing session for the staff, creating a safe space for them to express their emotions and share memories of Sarah. They lead a memorial service in the hospital chapel, allowing staff to honor Sarah's life and find closure. The chaplain also offers individual counseling sessions for those needing additional support.

Outcome:

The staff feels supported and connected through the shared mourning process. The memorial service provides a sense of closure and honors Sarah's contributions. Individual counseling helps staff members process their grief and return to their duties with renewed strength.

Analysis:

- Debriefing and Support: Providing a space for staff to share their emotions and memories facilitated collective healing.

- Memorial Service: Conducting a memorial service honored Sarah's life and provided closure for the staff.

- Ongoing Support: Offering individual counseling addressed the diverse needs of staff members, helping them cope with their grief.

Conclusion

These case studies illustrate the diverse and complex scenarios chaplains may encounter in their work. By applying the concepts discussed in this book—such as spiritual assessment, ethical decision-making, crisis intervention, facilitating religious rituals, and self-care—chaplains can effectively support patients, families, and healthcare staff. These real-life scenarios demonstrate the profound impact of compassionate and holistic spiritual care in healthcare settings, highlighting the essential role of chaplains in providing comfort, guidance, and support.

CONCLUSION

The integration of faith and medicine is a vital component of holistic healthcare. This book has explored various aspects of chaplaincy in healthcare settings, emphasizing the importance of spiritual care in addressing the comprehensive needs of patients, families, and healthcare staff. This concluding chapter summarizes the key points discussed and reinforces the significance of chaplains in providing compassionate, effective, and holistic care.

Summary of Key Points

1. The Role of a Hospital Chaplain

Hospital chaplains play a multifaceted role, providing spiritual care, emotional support, and ethical guidance. They work as integral members of the healthcare team, ensuring that patients' spiritual needs are met alongside their physical and emotional needs.

- Core Responsibilities: Chaplains provide spiritual care, emotional support, and ethical guidance to patients, families, and staff.

- Skills and Competencies: Key skills include active listening, empathy, cultural competence, and ethical decision-making.

2. Integrating Faith with Medical Care

Integrating faith with medical care involves addressing the spiritual needs of patients to promote overall well-being and recovery. Various models, such as the biopsychosocial-spiritual model, consider the physical, psychological, social, and spiritual dimensions of health.

- Importance of Spiritual Care: Spiritual care addresses the spiritual and emotional needs of patients, promoting holistic well-being.

- Collaboration with Healthcare Providers: Effective collaboration with healthcare providers is essential for integrating faith and medicine.

3. Spiritual Assessment and Care Planning

Conducting thorough spiritual assessments helps identify a patient's spiritual needs and resources. Developing a care plan based on these assessments ensures that spiritual interventions and support strategies are tailored to the patient's needs.

- Conducting Spiritual Assessments: Tools like the FICA and HOPE models help identify spiritual needs and resources.

- Developing Care Plans: Care plans should include spiritual interventions and support strategies tailored to the patient's needs.

4. Counseling Patients and Families

Chaplains provide essential counseling to patients and families, addressing issues such as fear, anxiety, grief, and existential questions. Effective counseling techniques include active listening, reflective listening, and validation.

- Addressing Specific Issues: Chaplains address issues like fear, anxiety, grief, and existential questions.

- Providing Comfort and Hope: Offering comfort and hope is central to the chaplain's role.

5. Interfaith and Multicultural Competence

Cultural competence involves recognizing and respecting cultural differences in beliefs, practices, and attitudes toward health and illness. Chaplains must be knowledgeable about various religious traditions and spiritual practices to provide appropriate and respectful care.

- Understanding Diverse Faiths: Knowledge of various religious traditions and spiritual practices is essential for providing appropriate care.

- Cultural Sensitivity: Cultural sensitivity promotes inclusivity and respect in healthcare settings.

6. Ethical and Moral Dilemmas in Healthcare

Chaplains often navigate ethical dilemmas involving end-of-life decisions, patient autonomy, and confidentiality. Ethical decision-making frameworks, such as the Four Principles Approach, guide chaplains in resolving these dilemmas.

- Common Ethical Issues: Ethical dilemmas in healthcare may involve end-of-life decisions, patient autonomy, and confidentiality.

- Ethical Decision-Making: Frameworks like the Four Principles Approach guide ethical decision-making.

7. Crisis Intervention and Trauma Support

Chaplains provide immediate emotional and spiritual support during crisis situations, helping patients, families, and healthcare staff navigate acute distress and trauma. Understanding the impact of trauma and providing trauma-informed care is essential.

- Crisis Response: Chaplains play a vital role in crisis situations, providing immediate support.

- Trauma-Informed Care: Understanding the impact of trauma and providing trauma-informed care is essential.

8. End-of-Life Care and Bereavement Support

End-of-life care involves providing comfort, dignity, and support to patients and their families. Chaplains offer spiritual guidance and facilitate religious rituals and practices that provide comfort and meaning.

- Supporting Patients and Families: End-of-life care focuses on providing comfort, dignity, and support.

- Rituals and Practices: Religious rituals and practices offer comfort and meaning during end-of-life care.

9. Self-Care for Chaplains

Self-care is crucial for chaplains to maintain their well-being and effectiveness. Strategies for self-care include regular reflection, supervision, peer support, and maintaining a healthy work-life balance.

- Importance of Self-Care: Self-care is essential for preventing burnout and maintaining well-being.

- Strategies for Self-Care: Strategies include regular reflection, supervision, peer support, and maintaining a healthy work-life balance.

10. Case Studies

Real-life case studies illustrate the challenges and successes chaplains may encounter in their work, demonstrating the application of concepts discussed in this book.

- Practical Examples: Case studies provide practical examples of chaplaincy in action.

- Key Learnings: Analyzing case studies highlights best practices and key learnings.

The Importance of Integrating Faith and Medicine

Integrating faith and medicine is essential for providing holistic care that addresses the comprehensive needs of patients. Spiritual care is a vital component of healthcare, promoting healing, well-being, and resilience. By incorporating spiritual care into medical practice, healthcare providers can offer more compassionate and effective care.

1. Holistic Healing

Holistic healing considers the physical, emotional, psychological, and spiritual dimensions of health. Integrating faith and medicine ensures that all aspects of a patient's well-being are addressed.

- Comprehensive Care: Holistic healing addresses the comprehensive needs of patients.

- Enhanced Well-Being: Spiritual care promotes overall well-being and recovery.

2. Compassionate Care

Compassionate care involves understanding and addressing the unique needs and experiences of each patient. Integrating faith and medicine fosters a compassionate approach to healthcare, enhancing patient satisfaction and outcomes.

- Empathy and Understanding: Compassionate care involves empathy and understanding of patients' experiences.

- Improved Outcomes: Compassionate care enhances patient satisfaction and health outcomes.

3. Collaboration and Teamwork

Effective integration of faith and medicine requires collaboration and teamwork among healthcare providers, chaplains, and patients. By working together, healthcare teams can provide more coordinated and comprehensive care.

- Interdisciplinary Collaboration: Collaboration among healthcare providers, chaplains, and patients is essential for integrated care.

- Coordinated Care: Teamwork ensures that care is coordinated and comprehensive.

Moving Forward

As healthcare continues to evolve, the integration of faith and medicine will remain crucial for providing holistic and compassionate care. Chaplains play a vital role in this integration, offering spiritual guidance, emotional support, and ethical leadership. By continuing to prioritize spiritual care, healthcare providers can ensure that patients receive the comprehensive support they need to heal and thrive.

1. Continued Education and Training

Ongoing education and training in spiritual care and cultural competence are essential for healthcare providers and chaplains. Staying informed about best practices and emerging research ensures that care remains effective and relevant.

- Professional Development: Continued education and training support professional growth and competency.

- Emerging Research: Staying informed about emerging research ensures that care remains effective and up-to-date.

2. Advocacy for Spiritual Care

Advocating for the inclusion of spiritual care in healthcare policies and practices is essential for promoting holistic care. Chaplains and healthcare providers can work together to highlight the importance of spiritual care and ensure it is integrated into healthcare systems.

- Policy Advocacy: Advocating for policies that support spiritual care in healthcare.

- Institutional Support: Ensuring that healthcare institutions prioritize and support spiritual care initiatives.

3. Building Support Networks

Building support networks among chaplains, healthcare providers, and faith communities strengthens the integration of faith and medicine. Collaboration and mutual support enhance the capacity to provide holistic care.

- Community Partnerships: Building partnerships with faith communities and support networks.

- Mutual Support: Collaboration and mutual support among healthcare providers and chaplains.

Conclusion

Integrating faith and medicine is essential for providing holistic, compassionate, and effective healthcare. Chaplains play a critical role in this integration, offering spiritual care that addresses the comprehensive needs of patients, families, and healthcare staff. By embracing the principles and practices discussed in this book, healthcare providers can ensure that patients receive the support and care they need to heal, thrive, and find meaning in their experiences. As we move forward, let us continue to prioritize the integration of faith and medicine, fostering a healthcare environment that honors the whole person and promotes holistic well-being.

FUTURE DIRECTIONS

As the field of hospital chaplaincy evolves, several emerging trends and future directions are shaping its development. These include increased interfaith collaboration, advances in spiritual care research, and the integration of new technologies. This chapter explores these trends and discusses their potential impact on the practice of hospital chaplaincy.

Increased Interfaith Collaboration

1. The Need for Interfaith Collaboration

With the growing diversity of patient populations, there is an increasing need for interfaith collaboration in hospital chaplaincy. This collaboration ensures that the spiritual needs of patients from various religious backgrounds are met respectfully and comprehensively.

- Diverse Patient Populations: Hospitals serve patients from a wide range of religious and cultural backgrounds.

- Inclusive Spiritual Care: Interfaith collaboration promotes inclusive and respectful spiritual care.

2. Strategies for Enhancing Interfaith Collaboration

To enhance interfaith collaboration, chaplains and healthcare institutions can implement several strategies.

- Interfaith Training: Provide chaplains with training in interfaith competencies, helping them understand and respect diverse religious practices and beliefs.

- Interfaith Teams: Establish interfaith chaplaincy teams that include representatives from various religious traditions.

- Community Partnerships: Build partnerships with local faith communities and religious leaders to support diverse spiritual needs.

3. Benefits of Interfaith Collaboration

Interfaith collaboration offers several benefits for patients, families, and healthcare providers.

- Comprehensive Care: Ensures that the spiritual needs of all patients are addressed, regardless of their religious background.

- Enhanced Understanding: Fosters mutual understanding and respect among chaplains and healthcare providers.

- Strengthened Support: Provides a broader support network for patients and families.

Advances in Spiritual Care Research

1. Importance of Spiritual Care Research

Research in spiritual care is essential for understanding its impact on patient outcomes and improving the practice of chaplaincy. Advances in this field can provide evidence-based insights that inform spiritual care practices and policies.

- Evidence-Based Practice: Research provides evidence to support the effectiveness of spiritual care interventions.

- Continuous Improvement: Ongoing research helps identify best practices and areas for improvement.

2. Key Areas of Research

Several key areas of research are driving advances in spiritual care.

- Impact on Patient Outcomes: Studies exploring the impact of spiritual care on patient outcomes, such as emotional well-being, recovery, and satisfaction with care.

- Best Practices: Research identifying best practices in spiritual care delivery, including effective interventions and approaches.

- Cultural Competence: Studies examining the role of cultural competence in spiritual care and its impact on patient experiences.

3. Implementing Research Findings

Integrating research findings into practice is crucial for advancing spiritual care.

- Training and Education: Incorporate research findings into chaplaincy training and education programs.

- Policy Development: Use research to inform the development of policies and guidelines for spiritual care.

- Quality Improvement: Apply research findings to enhance the quality and effectiveness of spiritual care services.

Integration of New Technologies

1. Role of Technology in Spiritual Care

Advances in technology are transforming the delivery of spiritual care in hospitals. Integrating new technologies can enhance access to spiritual resources, improve communication, and support innovative care approaches.

- Accessibility: Technology can make spiritual resources more accessible to patients and families.

- Communication: Digital tools can facilitate communication between chaplains, patients, and healthcare providers.

- Innovation: New technologies support innovative approaches to spiritual care.

2. Examples of Technological Integration

Several examples illustrate how new technologies are being integrated into spiritual care.

- Telechaplaincy: Providing spiritual care through video calls and telehealth platforms, especially for patients who cannot receive in-person visits.

- Digital Resources: Offering digital resources, such as prayer apps, online meditation guides, and virtual religious services.

- Electronic Health Records (EHRs): Integrating spiritual care documentation into EHRs to ensure comprehensive and coordinated care.

3. Challenges and Considerations

While technology offers many benefits, it also presents challenges and considerations.

- Privacy and Confidentiality: Ensuring that digital communication and records maintain patient privacy and confidentiality.

- Digital Literacy: Addressing varying levels of digital literacy among patients and staff.

- Balancing Technology and Personal Connection: Ensuring that technology complements, rather than replaces, personal interactions and relationships.

Emerging Roles and Specializations

1. Specialized Chaplaincy Roles

As the field of hospital chaplaincy evolves, new specialized roles and areas of expertise are emerging. These specializations allow chaplains to address specific needs and contexts more effectively.

- Palliative Care Chaplains: Specializing in providing spiritual care to patients with serious, life-limiting illnesses.

- Mental Health Chaplains: Focusing on the spiritual and emotional needs of patients with mental health conditions.

- Trauma Chaplains: Providing specialized care for patients and families affected by trauma and critical incidents.

2. Training and Certification

To support these emerging roles, new training and certification programs are being developed.

- Advanced Training: Offering advanced training programs in specialized areas of chaplaincy.

- Certification: Establishing certification processes to recognize and validate specialized expertise.

3. Collaboration with Other Disciplines

Specialized chaplains often collaborate closely with other healthcare disciplines to provide comprehensive care.

- Interdisciplinary Teams: Working as part of interdisciplinary teams to address complex patient needs.

- Integrated Care: Ensuring that spiritual care is integrated into overall patient care plans.

Future Challenges and Opportunities

1. Addressing Disparities in Spiritual Care

Ensuring equitable access to spiritual care for all patients remains a critical challenge. Efforts to address disparities include promoting cultural competence, expanding access to underserved populations, and advocating for inclusive policies.

- Equity and Inclusion: Promoting equity and inclusion in spiritual care practices and policies.

- Access: Expanding access to spiritual care for underserved and marginalized populations.

- Advocacy: Advocating for policies that support equitable and inclusive spiritual care.

2. Adapting to Changing Healthcare Environments

As healthcare environments continue to evolve, chaplains must adapt to new challenges and opportunities. This includes responding to changes in healthcare delivery models, addressing emerging health issues, and integrating new technologies and practices.

- Adaptability: Being adaptable and responsive to changes in healthcare environments.

- Innovation: Embracing innovation and new approaches to enhance spiritual care.

- Continuous Learning: Engaging in continuous learning and professional development to stay current with emerging trends and best practices.

3. Expanding Research and Evidence-Based Practice

Expanding research and evidence-based practice in spiritual care is essential for advancing the field. This includes fostering collaboration among researchers, practitioners, and institutions, and promoting the dissemination and implementation of research findings.

- Research Collaboration: Fostering collaboration among researchers, practitioners, and institutions.

- Evidence-Based Practice: Promoting the dissemination and implementation of research findings to enhance practice.

- Funding and Support: Advocating for funding and support for spiritual care research and initiatives.

Conclusion

The future of hospital chaplaincy is shaped by increased interfaith collaboration, advances in spiritual care research, and the integration of new technologies. These trends offer exciting opportunities for chaplains to enhance their practice and provide more comprehensive, compassionate, and effective care. As the field continues to evolve, chaplains must embrace these changes and continue to prioritize the spiritual, emotional, and cultural needs of patients, families, and healthcare staff. By doing so, chaplains will play a vital role in fostering holistic healthcare environments that honor and support the whole person.

RESOURCES AND FUTURE READING

Continued education and professional development are essential for chaplains to stay informed about best practices, emerging trends, and new research in the field of spiritual care. This chapter provides a list of recommended books, articles, and online resources that can support chaplains in their ongoing learning and development.

Recommended Books

1. Spiritual Caregiving: Integrating Body, Mind, and Spirit by Verna Benner Carson and Harold G. Koenig

- Overview: This book explores the integration of spiritual care with medical care, offering practical guidance for healthcare professionals.

- Topics Covered: Holistic care, spiritual assessment, and interventions.

2. The Practice of Pastoral Care: A Postmodern Approach by Carrie Doehring

- Overview: A comprehensive guide to pastoral care, this book addresses the complexities of providing spiritual care in contemporary settings.

- Topics Covered: Pastoral theology, counseling techniques, and ethical issues.

3. Professional Spiritual & Pastoral Care: A Practical Clergy and Chaplain's Handbook edited by Rabbi Stephen B. Roberts

- Overview: This handbook offers practical tools and insights for chaplains and clergy, covering a wide range of topics related to spiritual and pastoral care.

- Topics Covered: Crisis intervention, ethical dilemmas, and interfaith chaplaincy.

4. The Art of Presence: The Spiritual and Emotional Care of Those Who Are Ill by John Swinton

- Overview: Swinton's book emphasizes the importance of presence and deep listening in providing spiritual care to those who are ill.

- Topics Covered: Theological reflections, practical care techniques, and the role of presence in healing.

5. Caring for Those in Crisis: Facing Ethical Dilemmas with Patients and Families by Kenneth P. Mottram

- Overview: This book addresses the ethical dilemmas that chaplains often face and provides practical guidance for navigating these challenges.

- Topics Covered: Ethical decision-making, crisis intervention, and pastoral ethics.

6. The Wounded Healer: Ministry in Contemporary Society by Henri J.M. Nouwen

- Overview: Nouwen's classic book explores the role of the caregiver as a wounded healer, offering profound insights into the nature of pastoral care.

- Topics Covered: Theological reflections, pastoral care, and the caregiver's journey.

Recommended Articles

1. "The Role of the Healthcare Chaplain: A Literature Review" by M. Cadge and W. Sigalow

- Overview: This article provides a comprehensive review of the literature on the role of healthcare chaplains, highlighting key findings and trends.

- Publication: Journal of Health Care Chaplaincy

2. "Spiritual Care in Palliative Care: An Overview of the Literature" by J. Puchalski et al.

- Overview: An overview of the literature on spiritual care in palliative care settings, emphasizing the importance of integrating spiritual care into palliative care practices.

- Publication: Palliative Medicine

3. "Cultural Competence in Healthcare: Emerging Frameworks and Practical Approaches" by S. Betancourt et al.

- Overview: This article explores emerging frameworks and practical approaches for enhancing cultural competence in healthcare settings.

- Publication: Journal of Healthcare Management

4. "Trauma-Informed Care: A Sociocultural Perspective" by K. M. Fallot and M. Harris

- Overview: The article provides an overview of trauma-informed care from a sociocultural perspective, offering practical guidelines for implementation.

- Publication: American Journal of Orthopsychiatry

5. "The Impact of Spiritual Care on Patient Outcomes: A Systematic Review" by G. R. Fitchett et al.

- Overview: A systematic review of the literature examining the impact of spiritual care on various patient outcomes.

- Publication: Journal of Religion and Health

Online Resources

1. Association of Professional Chaplains (APC)

- Website: www.professionalchaplains.org

- Overview: APC offers resources, certification programs, and continuing education opportunities for chaplains.

2. The Center for Spirituality and Health at Mount Sinai

- Website: www.spiritualityandhealth.org

- Overview: This center provides resources, research, and education on the integration of spirituality and health.

3. Spiritual Care Association (SCA)

- Website: www.spiritualcareassociation.org

- Overview: SCA offers resources, training, and certification for spiritual care providers.

4. Journal of Health Care Chaplaincy

- Website: www.tandfonline.com/toc/whcc20/current

- Overview: A peer-reviewed journal that publishes research, reviews, and practical articles related to health care chaplaincy.

5. National Association of Catholic Chaplains (NACC)

- Website: www.nacc.org

- Overview: NACC offers resources, certification, and support for Catholic chaplains and spiritual care providers.

6. HealthCare Chaplaincy Network (HCCN)

- Website: www.healthcarechaplaincy.org

- Overview: HCCN provides resources, education, and research on the integration of chaplaincy and health care.

Continuing Education and Professional Development

1. CPE (Clinical Pastoral Education) Programs

- Overview: CPE programs provide experiential education for chaplains, focusing on the development of pastoral care skills.

- Organizations Offering CPE: Association for Clinical Pastoral Education (ACPE), National Association of

Catholic Chaplains (NACC), and the College of Pastoral Supervision and Psychotherapy (CPSP).

2. Workshops and Conferences

- Overview: Attending workshops and conferences provides opportunities for learning, networking, and professional development.

- Notable Conferences: APC Annual Conference, SCA Annual Conference, and various regional chaplaincy conferences.

3. Online Courses and Webinars

- Overview: Online courses and webinars offer flexible learning opportunities on a variety of topics related to spiritual care and chaplaincy.

- Providers: APC, SCA, and various academic and healthcare institutions.

Continued education and professional development are vital for chaplains to stay informed and effective in their roles. The resources and further reading materials provided in this chapter offer valuable insights, knowledge, and tools to support chaplains in their ongoing journey of learning and growth. By engaging with these resources, chaplains can enhance their skills, stay current with emerging trends and research, and continue to provide compassionate and holistic care to patients, families, and healthcare staff.

PROFESSIONAL ORGANIZATIONS

Professional organizations play a crucial role in supporting chaplains by providing resources, education, certification, and a community of peers. These organizations help chaplains stay informed about best practices, engage in continuous professional development, and connect with others in the field. This chapter provides information on key professional organizations that offer support and resources for chaplains.

Association of Professional Chaplains (APC)

1. Overview

The Association of Professional Chaplains (APC) is a national organization that certifies and supports professional chaplains across various settings, including healthcare, military, corrections, and more. APC promotes professional excellence in chaplaincy through certification, education, advocacy, and research.

2. Key Services and Resources

- Certification: APC offers board certification for chaplains who meet rigorous standards of education, experience, and competency.

- Continuing Education: APC provides a range of continuing education opportunities, including webinars, workshops, and conferences.

- Resources: The organization offers numerous resources, such as publications, research articles, and practice guidelines.

- Advocacy: APC advocates for the recognition and integration of spiritual care in healthcare and other institutions.

- Community: APC fosters a community of professional chaplains, providing networking opportunities and peer support.

3. Contact Information

- Website: www.professionalchaplains.org

- Email: info@professionalchaplains.org

- Phone: (847) 240-1014

National Association of Catholic Chaplains (NACC)

1. Overview

The National Association of Catholic Chaplains (NACC) supports and certifies Catholic chaplains and promotes the integration of pastoral care in healthcare, corrections, and other settings. NACC emphasizes the importance of spiritual care and the Catholic faith in chaplaincy practice.

2. Key Services and Resources

- Certification: NACC offers certification for Catholic chaplains, ensuring they meet specific standards of education, formation, and pastoral competency.

- Education: NACC provides continuing education opportunities, including conferences, webinars, and workshops focused on Catholic pastoral care.

- Resources: The organization offers resources such as publications, educational materials, and spiritual care guidelines.

- Advocacy: NACC advocates for the inclusion of spiritual care in healthcare and other settings, highlighting the unique contributions of Catholic chaplains.

- Community: NACC fosters a supportive community for Catholic chaplains, offering opportunities for networking and peer support.

3. Contact Information

- Website: www.nacc.org

- Email: info@nacc.org

- Phone: (414) 483-4898

Spiritual Care Association (SCA)

1. Overview

The Spiritual Care Association (SCA) is an international organization that supports spiritual care providers in healthcare and other settings. SCA focuses on advancing the quality and effectiveness of spiritual care through education, certification, advocacy, and research.

2. Key Services and Resources

- Certification: SCA offers certification for spiritual care providers, including chaplains, spiritual counselors, and other related roles.

- Education: SCA provides extensive educational resources, including online courses, webinars, and workshops on various aspects of spiritual care.

- Resources: The organization offers a wide range of resources, such as best practice guidelines, research publications, and educational materials.

- Advocacy: SCA advocates for the recognition and integration of spiritual care in healthcare and other settings.

- Community: SCA fosters a global community of spiritual care providers, offering networking opportunities and peer support.

3. Contact Information

- Website: [www.spiritualcareassociation.org](http://www.spiritualcarea ssociation.org)

- Email: info@spiritualcareassociation.org

- Phone: (212) 644-1111

Association for Clinical Pastoral Education (ACPE)

1. Overview

The Association for Clinical Pastoral Education (ACPE) is a national organization that provides clinical pastoral education (CPE) programs for chaplains and spiritual care providers. ACPE focuses on experiential education and professional development in pastoral care.

2. Key Services and Resources

- CPE Programs: ACPE offers accredited CPE programs that provide hands-on training and supervision in clinical settings.

- Certification: ACPE certifies CPE supervisors and educators who meet specific educational and professional standards.

- Education: ACPE provides educational resources and opportunities for professional development in pastoral care.

- Resources: The organization offers resources such as publications, research articles, and best practice guidelines.

- Community: ACPE fosters a community of pastoral educators and students, providing networking opportunities and peer support.

3. Contact Information

- Website: www.acpe.edu

- Email: acpe@acpe.edu

- Phone: (404) 320-1472

College of Pastoral Supervision and Psychotherapy (CPSP)

1. Overview

The College of Pastoral Supervision and Psychotherapy (CPSP) is an international organization that provides accreditation, certification, and support for pastoral counselors, chaplains, and psychotherapists. CPSP emphasizes the integration of pastoral and clinical care.

2. Key Services and Resources

- Certification: CPSP offers certification for pastoral counselors, chaplains, and clinical pastoral supervisors.

- Accreditation: The organization accredits training programs in pastoral care and counseling.

- Education: CPSP provides continuing education opportunities, including workshops, conferences, and webinars.

- Resources: CPSP offers resources such as publications, research articles, and practice guidelines.

- Community: CPSP fosters a supportive community for pastoral care providers, offering networking opportunities and peer support.

3. Contact Information

-Website: www.cpsp.org

- Email: info@cpsp.org

- Phone: (212) 246-6410

HealthCare Chaplaincy Network (HCCN)

1. Overview

The HealthCare Chaplaincy Network (HCCN) is a national organization that provides resources, education, and advocacy for chaplains and spiritual care providers in healthcare settings. HCCN focuses on integrating spiritual care into healthcare delivery.

2. Key Services and Resources

- Education: HCCN offers educational programs, including online courses, webinars, and conferences on various aspects of spiritual care.

- Resources: The organization provides resources such as research publications, best practice guidelines, and educational materials.

- Advocacy: HCCN advocates for the inclusion of spiritual care in healthcare policies and practices.

- Community: HCCN fosters a community of healthcare chaplains, offering networking opportunities and peer support.

3. Contact Information

- Website: www.healthcarechaplaincy.org

- Email: info@healthcarechaplaincy.org

- Phone: (212) 644-1111

National Association of Jewish Chaplains (NAJC)

1. Overview

The National Association of Jewish Chaplains (NAJC) supports and certifies Jewish chaplains, promoting the integration of Jewish spiritual care in healthcare, military, corrections, and other settings.

2. Key Services and Resources

- Certification: NAJC offers certification for Jewish chaplains, ensuring they meet specific standards of education and pastoral competency.

- Education: NAJC provides continuing education opportunities, including conferences, webinars, and workshops focused on Jewish pastoral care.

- Resources: The organization offers resources such as publications, educational materials, and spiritual care guidelines.

- Advocacy: NAJC advocates for the inclusion of Jewish spiritual care in healthcare and other settings.

- Community: NAJC fosters a supportive community for Jewish chaplains, offering opportunities for networking and peer support.

3. Contact Information

- Website: www.najc.org

- Email: info@najc.org

- Phone: (212) 632-4760

Professional organizations provide invaluable support, resources, and community for chaplains, enhancing their ability to provide effective and compassionate spiritual care. By engaging with these organizations, chaplains can access continuing education opportunities, certification programs, and a network of peers who share their commitment to holistic care. This chapter has provided an overview of key professional organizations in the field of chaplaincy, highlighting the services and resources they offer. As chaplains continue their journey of professional growth and development, these organizations will remain essential partners in their work to support patients, families, and healthcare staff.

APPENDICES

A STUDY QUESTIONS FOR EACH CHAPTER

Chapter 1: The Role of a Hospital Chaplain

1. What are the core responsibilities of a hospital chaplain?

2. How has the role of hospital chaplaincy evolved over the years?

3. Discuss the key skills and competencies required for effective chaplaincy.

Chapter 2: Integrating Faith with Medical Care

1. Why is spiritual care important in holistic healthcare?

2. Describe the biopsychosocial-spiritual model and its relevance to healthcare.

3. How can chaplains effectively collaborate with healthcare providers?

Chapter 3: Spiritual Assessment and Care Planning

1. What are the components of a thorough spiritual assessment?

2. How can tools like the FICA model be used in spiritual assessments?

3. Discuss the process of developing a spiritual care plan based on assessment findings.

Chapter 4: Counseling Patients and Families

1. What counseling techniques are most effective for chaplains?

2. How can chaplains address specific issues such as fear, anxiety, and grief?

3. Why is providing comfort and hope a central aspect of chaplaincy?

Chapter 5: Interfaith and Multicultural Competence

1. Why is cultural competence essential for chaplains?

2. Describe strategies for enhancing interfaith collaboration.

3. How can chaplains build relationships with diverse cultural and religious communities?

Chapter 6: Ethical and Moral Dilemmas in Healthcare

1. What are common ethical issues chaplains may encounter in healthcare settings?

2. Explain the Four Principles Approach to ethical decision-making.

3. How can chaplains facilitate ethical discussions among patients, families, and healthcare providers?

Chapter 7: Crisis Intervention and Trauma Support

1. What are the principles of effective crisis response?

2. How can chaplains provide trauma-informed care?

3. Discuss strategies for supporting patients, families, and healthcare staff during crises.

Chapter 8: End-of-Life Care and Bereavement Support

1. What are the key components of end-of-life care?

2. How can chaplains facilitate religious rituals and practices for patients and families?

3. Describe effective strategies for providing bereavement support.

Chapter 9: Self-Care for Chaplains

1. Why is self-care essential for chaplains?

2. Discuss various self-care practices for physical, emotional, and spiritual well-being.

3. How can chaplains integrate self-care into their daily routines?

Chapter 10: Case Studies

1. What are the key learnings from the provided case studies?

2. How can real-life scenarios help chaplains apply theoretical concepts?

3. Discuss the importance of reflection and analysis in improving chaplaincy practice.

Chapter 11: Future Directions

1. What are the emerging trends in hospital chaplaincy?

2. How can interfaith collaboration enhance spiritual care?

3. Discuss the impact of new technologies and research on the future of chaplaincy.

Chapter 12: Professional Organizations

1. Why are professional organizations important for chaplains?

2. Describe the key services and resources provided by organizations such as APC and NACC.

3. How can chaplains benefit from engaging with professional organizations?

Appendix B: Discussion Guides for Small Groups

Chapter 1: The Role of a Hospital Chaplain

- Discuss how the role of hospital chaplains has evolved and what this means for contemporary practice.

- Share personal experiences or observations about the skills and competencies that make an effective chaplain.

Chapter 2: Integrating Faith with Medical Care

- Explore the importance of spiritual care in promoting holistic health.

- Discuss ways to improve collaboration between chaplains and healthcare providers.

Chapter 3: Spiritual Assessment and Care Planning

- Role-play a spiritual assessment using the FICA model.

- Share experiences of developing and implementing spiritual care plans.

Chapter 4: Counseling Patients and Families

- Discuss challenges and successes in counseling patients and families.

- Share techniques that have been effective in providing comfort and hope.

Chapter 5: Interfaith and Multicultural Competence

- Discuss strategies for building cultural competence and understanding diverse faith traditions.

- Share experiences of interfaith collaboration and its impact on spiritual care.

Chapter 6: Ethical and Moral Dilemmas in Healthcare

- Explore common ethical dilemmas faced in healthcare and discuss potential resolutions.

- Discuss the application of the Four Principles Approach in real-life scenarios.

Chapter 7: Crisis Intervention and Trauma Support

- Share experiences of providing crisis intervention and trauma support.

- Discuss the importance of trauma-informed care and how to implement it effectively.

Chapter 8: End-of-Life Care and Bereavement Support

- Discuss the role of rituals and practices in end-of-life care.

- Share strategies for supporting families during bereavement.

Chapter 9: Self-Care for Chaplains

- Share self-care practices and strategies that have been effective.

- Discuss the challenges of maintaining a healthy work-life balance and how to overcome them.

Chapter 10: Case Studies

- Analyze the provided case studies and discuss key learnings.

- Share additional real-life scenarios and discuss how to apply theoretical concepts.

Chapter 11: Future Directions

- Discuss emerging trends in chaplaincy and their potential impact on practice.

- Explore opportunities for integrating new technologies and research into spiritual care.

Chapter 12: Professional Organizations

- Share experiences with professional organizations and their benefits.

- Discuss how to engage with professional organizations to enhance professional development.

Appendix C: Additional Resources on Hospital Chaplains

1. Books

- "Spiritual Caregiving: Integrating Body, Mind, and Spirit" by Verna Benner Carson and Harold G. Koenig

- "The Practice of Pastoral Care: A Postmodern Approach" by Carrie Doehring

- "Professional Spiritual & Pastoral Care: A Practical Clergy and Chaplain's Handbook" edited by Rabbi Stephen B. Roberts

2. Articles

- "The Role of the Healthcare Chaplain: A Literature Review" by M. Cadge and W. Sigalow

- "Spiritual Care in Palliative Care: An Overview of the Literature" by J. Puchalski et al.

- "Cultural Competence in Healthcare: Emerging Frameworks and Practical Approaches" by S. Betancourt et al.

3. Online Resources

- Association of Professional Chaplains (APC): www.professionalchaplains.org

- Spiritual Care Association (SCA): www.spiritualcareassociation.org

- Journal of Health Care Chaplaincy: www.tandfonline.com/toc/whcc20/current

4. Professional Organizations

- Association of Professional Chaplains (APC)

- Website: www.professionalchaplains.org

- National Association of Catholic Chaplains (NACC)

- Website: www.nacc.org

- Spiritual Care Association (SCA)

- Website: www.spiritualcareassociation.org

- Association for Clinical Pastoral Education (ACPE)

- Website: www.acpe.edu

- College of Pastoral Supervision and Psychotherapy (CPSP)

- Website: www.cpsp.org

- HealthCare Chaplaincy Network (HCCN)

- Website: www.healthcarechaplaincy.org

- National Association of Jewish Chaplains (NAJC)

- Website: www.najc.org

These resources provide valuable support, education, and community for chaplains, enhancing their ability to provide effective and compassionate spiritual care. Engaging with these resources and organizations can help chaplains stay informed, develop professionally, and connect with a network of peers dedicated to holistic healthcare.

* 9 7 9 8 3 3 0 6 0 2 2 4 7 *